ASPATORE BOOKS

About Aspatore Books

The Biggest Names in Business Books & More....

www.Aspatore.com

Aspatore Books has become one of the leading business book publishers in record setting time by publishing an all-star cast of C-level (CEO, CTO, CFO, COO, CMO) leaders from over half the Fortune 100 companies and other leading executives. Aspatore Books publishes the Inside the Minds, Bigwig Briefs, ExecEnablers and Aspatore Business Review imprints in addition to other best selling non-fiction books. Aspatore Books is focused on infusing creativity, innovation and interaction into the book publishing industry and providing a heightened experience for readers worldwide. Aspatore Books focuses on publishing traditional print books, while our portfolio company, Big Brand Books focuses on developing areas within the book-publishing world. Aspatore Books is committed to providing our readers, authors, bookstores, distributors and customers with the highest quality books, book related services, and publishing execution available anywhere in the world.

About Big Brand Books

Big Brand Books assists leading companies and select individuals with book writing, publisher negotiations, book publishing, book sponsorship, worldwide book promotion and generating a new revenue stream from publishing. Services also include white paper, briefing, research report, bulletin, newsletter and article writing, editing, marketing and distribution. The goal of Big Brand Books is to help our clients capture the attention of prospective customers, retain loyal clients and penetrate new target markets by sharing valuable information in publications and providing the highest quality content for readers worldwide. For more information please visit www.BigBrandBooks.com or email jonp@bigbrandbooks.com.

INSIDE THE MINDS

Inside the Minds: Internet Lawyers

The Most Up To Date Handbook of Important Answers to Issues Facing Every Entrepreneur, Lawyer, and Anyone With a Web Site

ASPATORE BOOKS

Published by Aspatore Books, Inc.
For information on bulk orders, sponsorship opportunities or any other questions please email store@aspatore.com. For corrections, company/title updates, comments or any other inquiries please email info@aspatore.com.

First Printing, January 2001
10 9 8 7 6 5 4 3 2 1

ISBN 1-58762-006-5

Library of Congress Card Number: 00-111060

Cover design by Michael Lepera/Ariosto Graphics & James Weinberg

This book is printed on acid free paper.

A special thanks to Brigeth Rivera, Ted Juliano, Kirsten Catanzano, Susan Chernauskas, and Melissa Conradi

About Inside the Minds

Business Intelligence From Industry Insiders

Become a Part of *Inside the Minds*

Become a Reviewer, Suggest a Topic For an Upcoming Book, Nominate an Executive, Post Comments on the Topics Mentioned, Read Expanded Excerpts, Free Excerpts From Upcoming Books

www.InsideTheMinds.com

Inside the Minds was conceived in order to give readers actual insights into the leading minds of business executives worldwide. Because so few books or other publications are actually written by executives in industry, *Inside the Minds* presents an unprecedented look at various industries and professions never before available. Each chapter is comparable to a white paper and is a very future oriented look at where their industry/profession is heading. In addition, the *Inside the Minds* web site makes the reading experience interactive by enabling readers to post messages and interact with each other, become a reviewer for upcoming books, read expanded comments on the topics covered and nominate individuals for upcoming books. The *Inside the Minds* series is revolutionizing the business book market by publishing an unparalleled group of executives and providing an unprecedented introspective look into the leading minds of the business world.

ASPATORE BUSINESS REVIEW
Tear Out This Page and Mail or Fax To:

Aspatore Books, PO Box 883, Bedford, MA 01730
Or Fax To (617) 249-1970

Name:

Email:

Shipping Address:

City: State: Zip:

Billing Address:

City: State: Zip:

Phone:

Lock in at the Current Rates Today-Rates Increase Every Year
Please Check the Desired Length Subscription:

1 Year ($1,090) _____ 2 Years (Save 10%-$1,962) _____
5 Years (Save 20%-$4,360) _____ 10 Years (Save 30%-$7,630) _____
Lifetime Subscription ($24,980) _____

(If mailing in a check you can skip this section but please read fine print below and sign below)
Credit Card Type (Visa & Mastercard & Amex):

Credit Card Number:

Expiration Date:

Signature:

Would you like us to automatically bill your credit card at the end of your subscription so there is no discontinuity in service? (You can still cancel your subscription at any point before the renewal date.) Please circle: Yes No

***(Please note the billing address much match the address on file with your credit card company exactly)**

Terms & Conditions

We shall send a confirmation receipt to your email address. If ordering from Massachusetts, please add 5% sales tax on the order (not including shipping and handling). If ordering from outside of the US, an additional $51.95 per year will be charged for shipping and handling costs. All issues are paperback and will be shipped as soon as they become available. Sorry, no returns or refunds at any point unless automatic billing is selected, at which point you may cancel at any time before your subscription is renewed (no funds shall be returned however for the period currently subscribed to). Issues that are not already published will be shipped upon publication date. Publication dates are subject to delay-please allow 1-2 weeks for delivery of first issue. If a new issue is not coming out for another month, the issue from the previous quarter will be sent for the first issue. For the most up to date information on publication dates and availability please visit www.Aspatore.com.

Inside the Minds:
Internet Lawyers

The Most Up To Date Handbook of Important Answers to Issues Facing Every Entrepreneur, Lawyer, and Anyone With a Web Site

CONTENTS

HARRISON SMITH

Traditional Legal Matters on the Internet

Krooth & Altman LLP

Partner

Common Mistakes Internet Startups Make From a Legal Standpoint

The mistakes that we see most frequently in early stage companies are overconfidence and being in too much of a hurry. The two are related.

Overconfidence is a direct result of the last several years when there were too many stories of Internet millionaires whose fortunes were based on business models that made no sense or businesses that simply were not really ready for the market. Everyone has read about or knows of someone who came up with an idea, wrote a "business plan" on a napkin, got millions of dollars in VC funding and took the company public, all with no real idea of how they were going to make money. Some entrepreneurs therefore believe that all they need to do is come up with an idea, put it on paper, submit it to a VC and pick up a million dollar check. (In some cases they have been right!) The stock market correction has thankfully disabused some people of these notions, but we still see lots of people chasing this model.

It is important to note that there is a world of difference between "very confident" and "overconfident," though the line can be tough to recognize. An entrepreneur needs to be very confident in their idea and in his/her ability to bring the idea to fruition. An entrepreneur must be able to persevere when all around them think that they are nuts and when every avenue to developing the business seems like a dead end. Only lots of confidence and passion can provide the entrepreneur with the strength to continue on when the odds of success seem insurmountable. A successful entrepreneur has that confidence and that passion and at the same time can tell when they become irrational.

The overconfident entrepreneur becomes wedded to their business and their model and believes absolutely that they will succeed. Overconfidence leads directly to a number of bad results:

1) The overconfident entrepreneur does not listen to constructive criticism and fails to act to refine his/her business to reflect such criticism.

2) The overconfident entrepreneur does not see changes in the marketplace and adapt accordingly.

3) The overconfident entrepreneur cannot evaluate their own model and see objectively the weaknesses in it that need to be addressed.

4) The overconfident entrepreneur underestimates the competition and/or deludes him/herself into believing that they have no competition. (Free advice – Never tell anyone that you have no competition. If you think that you have no competition or potential competition either: 1) you are simply too blind to see the competition or 2) your idea is so bad that no one else is foolish to pursue it. Every good idea generates competition).

5) The overconfident entrepreneur believes that everyone will immediately see the overwhelming value of the business and that the product/service will sell itself.

6) The overconfident entrepreneur reacts with hostility and frustration to rejection and is therefore not able to keep doors open for future business relationships and collaboration.

The second most important mistake that entrepreneurs make is being in too much of a hurry. The entrepreneur is so completely focused on the need for speed that they forgo the critical elements of planning and building a profitable business. Everything must be accomplished in "Internet time" regardless of whether the business is really ready. Like the overconfident entrepreneur, this entrepreneur believes that they have enough of a plan and enough of a business model and enough infrastructure in place to launch their business, seek funding, etc. They follow the "Ready, Fire Aim" model of building a business. Everything is always half-baked and implemented too soon, often with predictably dire results. There is no doubt that speed is important in today's economic environment. However, there is still such a thing as too much speed.

In the Internet economy the need to hurry and the need to be first can obscure some other needs: the need to research, understand and document your business, the need to move as far as you can on your own resources before approaching VCs, the need to find and engage the right team, the need to form partnerships and alliances, etc. The entrepreneur in too much of a hurry ignores all of these, at his/her peril. Your competitors will watch and learn from your mistakes, bring better offerings to customers and dominate your market. Remember that AOL was not the first ISP and Boeing did not market the first jet liners.

The most important advice that we give to clients stems from these two mistakes. We advise all of our clients to be realistic in their plans and in their evaluation of their potential. We advise them to be thorough, to plan and to be ready. Do we advise them to take it easy, sleep in and start work after lunch? Of course not. In fact, we advise them to bust their butts every hour of every day so that they will be ready for success. We tell them that they need to focus on the "4Ms and a P" in defining their business:

1) Management – Who is on the team, both actual management and advisors? Have they quit their day jobs and committed to the business?
2) Market – How large is it and how fast is it growing? How is it stratified? Who are the appropriate customers?
3) Money – How will they make money? How will they deploy the investment dollars that they seek? How much of their own money have they invested?
4) Milestones – What concrete accomplishments have they achieved in the business and what hurdles have they

surmounted? What evidence can they point to showing what they can reasonably be expected to accomplish? What partnerships do they have? What customers?
5) Product – Is it developed and ready to deploy or is it just an idea? Does it work?

We advise our clients to be constantly open to credible input. The most important characteristic for an early stage entrepreneur is intellectual honesty, the ability to objectively evaluate input from varied sources and respond accordingly. Good sources of input abound if the entrepreneur makes the effort to solicit it. We advise our clients to become actively involved in our local early stage technology community so that they can meet people and obtain that input by learning from the experiences of others. We advise them to take advantage of all of the local government, university and business programs available to help them to evaluate their ideas. We advise them not to become too wedded to their ideas and to be ready to change when they see an opportunity, or when they see an error that needs to be addressed. We advise them that an entrepreneur must be ever alert to indulging in too much ego gratification. Admit mistakes quickly, address the error and move on. The odds are that the eventual business will deviate substantially from the original business plan. The best entrepreneurs can tell when something is not working and change quickly. That is why VCs always say that they are more interested in funding great management teams than great business plans.

Another critical piece of information that we give to our clients is to make the most use they can of strategic relationships. In today's economy no one is going it alone. Everyone needs to try and leverage off of the strengths and successes of others. It takes too long and costs too much to build for yourself what someone else has already and will be glad to license to you. We also advise them that strategic relationships come in all shapes and sizes. Informal collaboration with someone in a related business is a great way to gain market intelligence, sales leads, etc. Joint marketing is often easy to do and allows two companies to leverage one sales effort directed at the same customers. Collaboration opportunities are all around if the entrepreneur gets out in the community and actively seeks them out. The virtual company is a reality. Devote your efforts to what you do best and to what is truly core to your business. Outsource other functions to companies to which those functions are core.

Legal Changes That Will Affect Companies Doing Business on the Internet

Most of the legal concepts applicable to the brick and mortar world have translated into the online world without the need for major surgery. Many of the changes that we have seen and will see in the near future are changes made to aid the application of the existing laws to new forms of doing business in the online world. For example, for companies doing business on the Internet, a contract is still a contract. The parties are still required to conform to the terms of the contract and if they fail to do so, they are exposed to lawsuits for noncompliance, nonperformance, etc. However, in the computer age, not every contract will be on paper and signed with a pen, so the law must come up with a way to accommodate this new form of communicating and forming contracts. This is not unlike the changes wrought by the advent of the copying machine and the fax machine. The law needs to adapt to new forms of transactions so that the basic substantive laws can be applied.

International Issues

The first change in the laws that impact Internet companies is the simple fact that there is no geography on the Internet. Once launched, a Web site can be accessible in every state in the U.S. and every country on earth.

Traditional companies needed to define the geographic area within which they would operate and learn and comply with the laws in that area. It was relatively easy to avoid doing business in states or countries where the laws were perceived to impose too great a burden. The company could avoid sending salesmen there, making sales calls, shipping product, etc. The company could fairly easily track where it was doing business, where their sale leads and customers came from and where its marketing messages would be received. If your product or service was illegal in France, you simply did not sell it there.

Internet companies cannot so easily limit their businesses to defined geographic areas. The Web is global by definition. It is extremely difficult to identify the people with whom you are dealing and the geographic area from which they are contacting you. It is difficult to deny access to your site based on a set of geographic parameters. That being the case, Internet companies are often inadvertently exposed to the jurisdiction and the laws of other states in the U.S. and other countries abroad. Many of these jurisdictions may impose rules and regulations that the company has not considered in structuring its business model, product offerings, marketing message, etc. What is perfectly legal at home may turn out to be criminal in a foreign country, as some Internet companies have already learned the hard way. The off-line world has a set of well-developed rules to determine what law applies to a particular transaction and whether a party can be held accountable in a foreign jurisdiction. In the online world lawyers, lawmakers and courts are all trying to figure out what laws apply when a Web site owned by a company based in California and hosted on servers in Barbados is viewed by a customer in Germany. So far, there are no uniform answers and businesses are definitely at risk.

In addition to the legal matters, the company also needs to consider culture, language, etc. in structuring its business to operate globally. What works in the U.S. may be considered not only bad business in foreign countries but may be rude, insulting, etc. according to local custom and usage. Some companies address this issue by putting up different Web sites for different countries, translating all of the material into multiple languages and policing the material for compliance with local standards of conduct and commerce. Others use a single Web site and try to walk a middle ground in putting up content that will be acceptable and effective in the greatest number of jurisdictions. Some simply translate content into the local language and don't worry about local custom. Whatever the decision, the process is difficult, expensive and involves various risks for the eventual success of the business.

New Issues Surrounding Contracts in the Online World

A contract formed on the Internet is still a contract and is subject to all of the laws applicable to contracts generally. However, there are questions as to when a contract has actually been formed. In the off-line world we know that the rule requires an offer by one party and acceptance by the other party in order to form a binding contract. We know that the offer or the acceptance can be written or verbal and the contract can be written or verbal. The law has had many years to refine the concepts of what constitutes offer and acceptance. For example, in the offline world we know that an offer has been accepted and a contract formed when that acceptance has been placed in the mail. We have rules that govern required disclosures of relevant information and assure that neither party is being misled and that the contract should therefore be enforced.

In the online world the parties may never deal with each other face to face, verbally or by exchange of correspondence. We have new potential models of offer and acceptance and exchange of information to be considered and dealt with. Should a "click wrap" contract be enforceable? Does it constitute acceptance when a person clicks on the "Accept" button, thereby forming an enforceable contract? What if the person has not been provided with a full copy of the contract that they are allegedly accepting? In the area of boxed software, what is the effect of the "shrink wrap" contract and the customer's "acceptance" by opening the package (especially given that the terms of the contract being accepted are inside the box and have not even been seen by the accepting party). How can the parties each be assured access to information concerning the contract being formed and that such information is not misleading?

The online world also places great reliance on a Web site visitor accepting the site's terms and conditions of use and service. These terms and conditions are intended to form a binding contract between the Web site operator and the Web site user, governing all aspects of their interaction. How does the site visitor evidence that acceptance so as to contractually bind him/herself to abide by those terms and conditions? Surely you cannot ask every visitor to your Web site to read and accept the full terms and conditions. Is it enough to post a link on the site giving the visitor access to the terms and conditions should they choose to read them? How prominent a link? What about visitors that enter the site other than through the home page and may therefore miss link to the terms and conditions altogether? Should they be bound? Again, this is simply a matter of figuring out how to apply the old, off-line rules of offer and acceptance to the new, online communication medium. It is not a radical new law substantively, but just an attempt to fit new models of behavior into the existing legal framework.

The Future of Online Contracts

Another area in which the law needs to adapt so that the old rules can apply to the new behavior models is the area of so-called paperless contracting. In the off-line world there are a variety of laws that require that certain contracts must be in writing in order to be enforceable. These laws apply to contracts entered into between parties in particular substantive areas, providing for particular services to be provided, etc. and the laws vary somewhat from jurisdiction to jurisdiction. The law must now find a way to allow for contracts to be formed electronically and still be enforceable notwithstanding the existence of these various laws. Failure to do so will severely hamper the growth of electronic commerce and the efficiency engendered by that growth.

In order to allow for paperless contracts, there are a variety of practical and legal matters that need to be addressed. For example, if the contract is not to be on paper, how will it be memorialized? What record will the parties have of what they actually agreed to if they do not have the actual signed contract in their files? How will they be assured that an electronic contract has not been tampered with while stored on a disk or otherwise? How will the parties prove that the contract was in fact "signed" by both parties? How will we deal with special circumstances like mortgages that have traditionally been recorded in local government offices? Technology has been addressing each of these issues and answers are now available, though no standards have yet emerged.

The legal response to this issue has been interesting and follows the model of making minimal changes to laws necessary to accommodate new modes of communication and new business models rather than making substantive changes to existing laws. Rather than making far reaching substantive changes to the array of existing laws on this issue, Congress and the states (in adopting the proposed model statutes) have taken the approach of simply stating that an electronic contract is to be given the same weight as a written contract. The federal E-Sign statute and the state UETA and UCITA statutes, taken together will provide a framework for the formation of electronic contracts. The two state laws have not yet been widely enacted and there is differing opinion as to when, or whether, they will become widespread.

Another issue facing lawmakers in adapting the legal system to changing modes of communication has been whether, or how, to define the new technologies and the new ways that contracts can be formed in the absence of paper and ink signatures. The current laws have remained technology agnostic, electing not to require or encourage any particular form of technology to be used in contract formation. Again, the laws have stayed fairly true to the existing legal precedents. The laws largely allow the parties to decide what modes of offer and acceptance are acceptable in any particular situation. This approach not only has the benefit of retaining familiar legal concepts, but provides a framework that will hopefully be flexible enough to adapt to the next wave of technology when it arrives, as it surely will.

Intellectual Property Issues

One of the most basic functions of the Internet is to serve as a medium for the collection and distribution of information. The laws of intellectual property touch all aspects of Internet operations. Again, the existing laws are equally applicable to the Web and must simply be considered in the light of new communications modes and new business models.

Copyright law protects works of original authorship fixed in any tangible medium of expression. It is not necessary for a copyright to be registered to be effective, though there are substantial benefits to registering your copyright. Indeed, all that is necessary is the act of creation and fixing in tangible medium. In general, the copyright is owned by the author of the material, subject to certain exceptions such as works made for hire, which governs works created by employees and certain contractors, and that ownership gives the author various exclusive rights to reproduce the work, prepare derivative works, distribute copies, perform the work and display the work. If anyone other than the author does any of those things, the copyright has been violated, again subject to limited exceptions, such as "fair use," which allows limited use for educational purposes for example. Posting material on a Web site can clearly be a violation of copyright laws if the Web site owner does not have proper authority from the copyright owner.

One of the central business models of Web based businesses is that everyone collaborates, licenses, outsources, etc. in building their sites. Few and far between are those sites that create in house everything that they put up on the Web and all of the software infrastructure supporting the Web site. That being the case, the first practical issue facing a Web based business is deciding whether and to what extent it can legally use information, code or tools provided by third parties. For example, if a company purchases content from a third party, what assurances can be obtained that such third party actually has the right to license such information and material. This analysis is the same as that which would be undertaken by an offline publisher. By publishing such content you are potentially exposing your company to suit for copyright infringement. In order to mitigate that risk, it is important to do careful diligence on the parties from whom you obtain content and to obtain from them appropriate representations and warranties regarding their right to provide the content to you, as well as indemnification in case it turns out that they in fact lacked such authority.

On the flip side of this issue, what can you do to protect your own rights if you are the copyright owner? Once you license content to a Web site, how can you be certain that the content will be used in the contemplated manner, that it will not be distributed to others for publication or distributed through unintended channels? As shown in the Napster case, on the Web, content can flow freely and potentially outside of the control of the copyright owner. You need to be careful whom you deal with and be sure that your agreements are written with enough specificity to define what the content licensee may and may not do with your content. Try and retain rights with regard to how the content is displayed and to limit the channels through which the content may be distributed.

Related to the issue of copyright infringement in posting content, is the issue of copyright infringement in the use of the software infrastructure that supports your Web site. Odds are that you contracted with an outside firm to build your Web site. You probably do not know where they got the software. Is it off the shelf, something that they developed in house or something that they had prepared by a third party contractor? It is possible that your developer has infringed upon the copyright of third parties by providing that software to you, and that you could be held liable for further violations. As is true of content, it is important to do adequate due diligence and to obtain appropriate representations, warranties and indemnifications.

Another issue of concern to a Web site owner is whether and to what extent the use of links, framing, etc. may carry copyright implications. Framing may very well be held to be a copyright infringement as the Web site is arguably publishing material to which it has no rights. The posting of links to material may be considered to be a contributory infringement of copyright if the material is being published in violation of someone else's copyright, or you may be held to have endorsed the material as reliable, accurate, etc. Policing of all of the material passing through one's Web site would be nearly impossible, yet the risk of liability for copyright infringement based upon such material is very real. In part you can mitigate this risk through your terms of service and use by making clear that links are provided for user convenience only and that the site does not in any way recommend or endorse the content or warrant its ownership.

Recently, the Digital Millennium Copyright Act has alleviated some of these concerns by codifying certain exceptions and protections for the posting of information and material by passive "service providers." Passive information providers are protected from liability as long as they meet the definitions of a "service provider" and put in place various procedures to allow for the termination of copyright infringement through its Web site. However, these protections are not available to everyone, so it is important to monitor the information you post on your site and to be extremely careful to document your rights to use whatever materials you post and to obtain indemnifications wherever possible from the providers of the material.

Changes in the Legal Industry in the Future

The changes in the legal industry have been evidenced in those portions of the industry that work with new technology companies, a fairly small part of the legal industry overall. The bulk of the attorneys working in this specialty were involved in other areas in years past, as the early stage technology had not yet experienced its explosive growth and need for attorneys. As more attorneys have shifted into this area of practice they have to some extent had to learn new ways of doing business and adapted to the life and work styles of technology clients. A good example is the lack of formality in the technology industry that has led to increasing informality in the demeanor and attire of lawyers. Another good example is the extremely fast pace of the technology industry and the fact that it runs 24/7, which has required more lawyers to carry laptops, pagers and cellular phones so that they are available at all hours of the day and night.

For those of us who do represent these companies, there are a number differences between this practice and the representation of more established companies. The first and most important major difference is also a major benefit: the work that we do for our early stage clients is broadly based and extremely important to their success, often more so than is the case with more established companies. We are able to get involved in all aspects of their business, to see the "big picture" and to render advice across the entity. With our very early stage clients in particular, we are as likely to be advising on business strategy, marketing and product as we are to be drafting contracts or negotiating transactions. In our office, we try to limit the number of our clients so that we have the time and the ability to become deeply involved in the business of each of those clients.

Another change is that things change very rapidly in the business of these clients. It is not uncommon for the client's business to completely change virtually overnight as an ineffective business model or market is discarded in favor of a new one. As attorneys, we need to adapt as rapidly as our clients adapt. When new opportunities arise, we need to be ready to help the client to take advantage of those opportunities, and quickly. We need to understand the client's business, their industry and all of their relationships so that we can help them to adapt and change quickly.

Another change is less positive: early stage companies are by their nature short of funds and the lawyer needs to be careful to make appropriate arrangements for compensation. Many different models have evolved, from those attorneys who simply bill by the hour and expect to be paid regularly to those attorneys who have agreed to work in return for equity and those in the middle who have agreed to defer part of their fee in return for other compensation. The attorney must be careful in choosing clients and must make a determination of the likelihood that the business will be successful and will be able to pay the legal fees that are incurred. This can often be a difficult determination to make. In effect, attorneys must try and evaluate clients the same way that a venture capitalist would. Part of the attorney's consideration is whether the company will be able to obtain VC funding or otherwise grow and become successful. Additionally, there can be significant attrition in early stage clients, so again the attorney needs to be somewhat selective.

A final change worth noting relates to the very early stage companies with which we work. Because they often lack resources, we need to be very involved in helping them to put together all of the elements needed to build a business. When they come to us, the entire business may be only one person, so we need to help them find personnel resources. They may not have a formal business plan, so we need to help them to write the business plan. They generally are in need of funding, so we devote substantial efforts to getting them ready for funding and to helping them find the appropriate investors for their company.

Harrison Smith is a graduate of Cornell University and the Duke University School of Law. He has been with Krooth & Altman LLP (www.krooth.com) since 1979 and serves as a managing partner of the firm. Mr. Smith's practice is devoted primarily to representing early stage technology companies, providing counsel on a broad range of legal issues as well as general business counseling. He is himself an entrepreneur, having started and run a business providing patented products for the ski industry. In addition to his work on behalf of entrepreneurs, Mr. Smith provides services to local business support organizations including Virginia's Center for Innovative Technology, the Northern Virginia Technology Council and the Technology Resource Alliance, and provides services for various venture-funding events. He serves as counsel to the National Minority Technology Council and the Virginia Minority Technology Council. Mr. Smith lectures frequently on issues relating to early stage technology companies and he is currently writing a book on the process of obtaining venture capital.

CARL COHEN

Challenges for Internet & Technology Companies

Buchanan Ingersoll

Co-Chairman of Technology and Entrepreneurial Services Group

Background

I've been working with technology companies for over 22 years. Early on in my career, at a time when very few professional services firms paid any attention to this area, I started focusing on young entrepreneurial growth companies. I found it very exciting to practice law in this area because of the opportunity to work hand in hand with entrepreneurs, the management team and other key people involved in building the company. I could apply a broader set of skills, beyond my legal skills, to help entrepreneurs grow successful companies. As an advisor to entrepreneurial growth companies, you operate as a quasi-member of the management team. And for me, there was and continues to be a lot of excitement in being involved with those kinds of companies and tremendous gratification in helping them be successful.

Biggest Issues Facing Clients

One of the biggest issues is human capital. More specifically, I think the biggest challenge companies face is finding the right people to develop the business model or strategy, execute the operating plan and respond to unanticipated complications. What is absolutely essential to a company's growth is having people with the ability to execute and make ideas work. It's really challenging to get the management team right as well.

The more direct answer is that the capital formation process has always been and continues to be a critical issue. Raising capital is a time consuming and distracting experience, yet it is of paramount importance that it be done correctly. Before the market correction, there was a period of time when raising capital was easier than it had traditionally been, valuations were higher and the playing field was tilted in favor of the entrepreneurs. There was a lot of money chasing deals. There's still a lot of money out there, but today it's much more challenging to raise that money.

The second answer is that while the legal issues must be addressed, I don't believe they constitute the main challenges young entrepreneurial technology companies face. If you have the right lawyers working effectively with the business and technical people, the legal issues can be managed.

Important Issues

One of the most important issues that still needs to be shaped is privacy rights. Whether it is a question of profiling, customer data, financial information or other sensitive personal information, we have only seen the tip of this issue. The Internet has permitted companies to compile information about consumer behavior, quicker and easier than ever before. In some cases, they can collect information that was previously unavailable. For many companies, the information and data produced or collected by the companies can be more valuable than the company's total revenues. Because in many respects this issue is viewed as a consumer protection issue, it is only a matter of time before the legislature addresses it by passing laws. And it is possible, with the Internet jurisdiction, for a company to face federal, state and international laws across the globe. I think that companies need to prepare for the onslaught of legislation that has already begun and will continue over the next few years. I would harbor a guess that companies that act reasonably and responsibly about protecting the interests of individuals will fair well through this storm.

Biggest Mistakes Being Made

One of the most critical decisions an entrepreneur makes is selecting the people who will direct the company's growth. Choosing the wrong people and failing to take corrective action quickly can really hurt a startup. The entrepreneur is building a business. Too often young companies that do not have the right people in place have to suffer significantly through the consequences of poor decisions made by those people. The technology is the tool for creating the business, not the business itself. Getting the right management team in place is a major determinant of a company's success.

Additionally, I have found many first time entrepreneurs have trouble knowing what to focus on, in terms of prioritizing. Early on, involvement by experienced professional advisors can significantly reduce the learning curve for a fast-moving entrepreneur who is trying to manage competing priorities.

Working With a New Internet Company

First, you want to protect whatever technology resides within the company. Whether you're talking about employees or consultants that have worked to build the technology, making sure that the intellectual property ownership has been transferred to the company is critical. It is also important to decide what intellectual property protection should be sought.

Number two, I look at the equity structure of the company. You need to make sure there are no ambiguities about who owns the company. You need to review how that ownership is allocated among the key players and the relationships among the key players. Sometimes the allocation isn't correct, and the time to correct it is sooner rather than later.

And finally, I assess the company's capital formation needs to determine how to position the company to prospective investors.

Issues Being Faced by Internet Companies

A lot of these issues have existed before, but speed is increasingly important. Entrepreneurs have got to be able to jump on opportunity and act on issues. As their advisors, you have to help them move very, very, quickly. Speed is life. That's probably the biggest difference.

Dealing With Issues

To some extent the issues are harder to deal with because the laws either do not exist or the existing laws did not contemplate the current state of technology. However, very few of the new developments in these laws have been surprising. Applying good business and legal judgment has enabled many companies to not only "predict" the way laws are shaping, but also to help shape those laws through industry practices. For example, "shrink-wrap" or "click-wrap" licenses have been used for many years, even when courts held them to be unenforceable. Now, years later, courts have held them to be an enforceable means of contracting between parties, and legislation has been adopted in certain states that further recognize this form of agreement, as it has become a industry standard for mass-market contracting.

Important Things That Need to be Addressed

The primary consideration is the protection of the company's technology. Non-compete agreements, to the extent that you can get them (because in a lot of markets you're not able to get them), should be considered. Other protective provisions like confidentiality agreements, agreements not to solicit customers or encourage other employees to leave the company, and a clause that assigns to the employer all inventions conceived by the employee are vehicles that can protect the company's intellectual property and proprietary information and should be addressed.

The other thing that's really important is the structure of the equity incentive plans. Equity incentive plans can be drivers to attract high quality executives who share your entrepreneurial spirit. Stock options and grants tied directly to future performance are tools to attract and retain talent.

Equity and Stock Option Plans

There are not tremendous variations but some companies are more innovative than others. A lot of times we use restricted stock as opposed to stock options, particularly for the top people. Restricted stock can often result in a beneficial tax treatment. You'll also see variations in the plans in terms of acceleration of the options vesting when the company is sold or goes public.

The Importance of Confidentiality Agreements

They are very important. There are situations where you do seek to enforce them, or frankly wish you had them to enforce. We just had a client that went through a trade secret problem where the prospective partner had come in and done due-diligence, and then someone from the prospective partner's team left and started a competing company. People who finance companies, the venture capitalists and so on, generally resist signing any confidentiality agreements. Prospective strategic partners may be more willing, depending on who it is. Companies like Yahoo and Microsoft might be very resistant, or if they sign them you might not get much protection. The employees of the company and the consultants should sign confidentiality agreements, particularly if they're in a technical area or are involved with sensitive information. Generally the confidentiality agreements can be enforced. It's a cost-benefit decision whether you ever would try to enforce it. Sometimes they can have the benefit of having a chilling affect on people who might seek to violate them.

Important Legal Issues to Address in Any Sort of Business Development Partnership

It's important to have a mutual understanding of each party's expectations. Companies need to clearly define their goals including the level of control they require, funding needs and marketing resources. It's important to have assurances that each party will devote certain resources and give the partnership priority in certain instances. Rights to future inventions, payment/royalty arrangements, protection of proprietary rights, confidentiality and cooperation or division of resources are all issues that need to be combed through very carefully. Performance is another issue. What happens if one party performs and the other doesn't? And there's the general issue of how a particular partnership affects the company's overall business model or business strategy. The partnership gives you certain benefits, but at what price? Are there any other provisions in the agreements that limit your future alternatives or upside potential as a company?

One Internet company that we represented partnered with one of the major portals at a time when it was in real need of a strategic partner. The portal was very interested in having certain rights to buy our client. So those provisions were very hotly negotiated. Every word was examined very carefully, because that kind of provision can limit any ability you have to market the company if you're trying to sell it or get competing bids to drive up the valuation. You have to be very careful about the price you might have to pay for the benefits you receive from the strategic partnership.

The Biggest Challenges Preventing Deals From Getting Done

The biggest challenges are overly aggressive positions that are outside of market terms or unrealistic expectations or demands. Communication is always an issue as well. If you have parties that are misreading or don't understand each other or each other's expectations, then it won't be a good business fit.

Entrepreneurs and their advisors need to be attentive to personality dynamics. Effective negotiating involves an understanding where the people on the other side of the table are coming from, their objectives, their decision-making process, and the issues that concern them. That understanding not only helps you assess your leverage, it clarifies whether the people across the table are a good fit with your company's vision and culture.

Best Ways to Negotiate Financial Terms When Raising Capitals

Generally the way you do this is to go into the marketplace and convince a number of different potential investors that this is a great venture, obtain alternative term sheets and negotiate from there. While there are different methodologies and people can argue over the financial projections of the company, valuation is still very subjective. Ultimately the marketplace speaks to that issue, and you want to interact with the marketplace in a manner that maximizes your valuation.

What Venture Capitalists Want

I don't think the basic structure of venture deals has changed, but the basic terms have changed as a result of the shakeup. The venture capitalists may be more aggressive, certainly on valuation and maybe on other terms that would enable them to address a situation where a company is not executing as expected. For example, we have seen venture capitalists more aggressive in requesting warrants that increase the venture capitalist's percentage ownership and possibly the control of the company in the event the company does not meet performance criterion. In the case of a staged financing, the venture capitalist may also require the company to achieve certain milestones before the additional money is invested.

Legal Issues for Internet Companies to Address

The continued development of copyright laws in the United States and abroad will be important to watch. Companies like Napster have highlighted the conflict between existing intellectual property laws and new forms of technology and business, such as peer-to-peer computing. Copyright laws will need to adapt to adequately protect the interests of authors but also to promote the sharing of information. This same issue applies to ownership of databases and collections of information.

Smaller Versus Bigger Companies

Larger companies, with more infrastructure and more experienced businesspeople will tend to use outside lawyers on pure legal issues.

Working with the younger companies requires you to not only take care of the legal issues, but also to proactively employ a broader set of business and financial skills. Younger companies need their lawyers to give them business, financial, legal and deal-making guidance. Growing companies have a disproportionate need for resources - you bring more to the table for them in terms of value adds like business advice and contacts.

Pressing Legal Issues for Younger Companies

Companies need to develop appropriate processes and methodologies for addressing legal issues as they grow. This is a business issue as much as a legal one. In the early stages, these companies sometimes take short cuts, improvise, etc., because resources are tight and the risk/reward analysis can support this approach. As the companies grow, so do their legal needs, as well as the number of people raising these issues. There comes a point in the company life cycle where, without appropriate processes for handling legal issues, a company can waste time and money, as different employees start to raise similar issues with different lawyers who are unaware of what other people are working on. As a company grows, and it is not just a few founders raising issues and asking the questions, it can become difficult for others in the company to know when to ask for legal advice and how to efficiently utilize service providers.

International Legal Issues to Address

As mentioned earlier, privacy laws are important to watch internationally. In fact, it was the European Union that really first highlighted this issue for the rest of us. Taxation on e-commerce transactions is another important issue, particularly since the tax regimes in other countries are so different than the United States. Intellectual property laws are also important to consider internationally. Whether it is patent, copyright, trademark or trade secrets, protecting rights in the United States do not guarantee protection in other countries. This is important in a borderless, Internet society. Encryption is also important. As companies try to protect their technology or information being transmitted over the Internet, there are specific rules and regulations that apply to the exportation of encryption technologies.

Important M&A Issues for the Entrepreneur

That's a situation where you generally do want a confidentiality agreement. Not withstanding that, you only want to disclose the information you feel necessary to get to the next step to see if the party is really interested and see what kind of terms they might consider. Confidentiality agreements are important to have, but litigation is the last place that you want to be if you're a young growing company. So you have to choose what information you give out very carefully, who you give it to, and the quality and trustworthiness of the people you're dealing with. Really examine where they're coming from, what their interests are, whether they're genuine or whether there are ulterior motives for extracting information from you.

Deal Making Strategies

There are certain key things. You have to have the best understanding you can of the parties that you're dealing with and what they're looking for, what their expectations are, what they think, and really try to put yourself in their shoes and see how they view the deal. That perception needs to be accurate, because if it's not accurate you could misfire.

Another important point is to understand your own client's expectations and interests and have a heart-to-heart discussion about that.

The third point is to understand the relative leverage of the parties. Ultimately the facts of the situation and the relative leverage of the parties are the real drivers in the outcome of a particular transaction. So you have to understand how much leverage you have, where it is, and how to utilize it.

You need to understand where particular transactions should come out in light of market terms and the relative leverage of the parties and then see the critical path for getting there. What are the major things that have to be put in place to get there? What are the hurdles and how are you going to overcome them?

Litigious Situations

You want to avoid spending the time and money on lawsuits, so you would want to try and intercede and see if there's a way of resolving the matter short of litigation. That may involve bringing additional personalities into the mix, whether it be lawyers or other business people or board members on both sides. Sometimes, over the course of a relationship people become too much at odds with each other to work something out. Other advisors or mediators can work with them to bring about a resolution.

Litigation is really a negotiation tool, a tool towards finding a resolution. You have to be innovative and creative to figure out if there's some other business solution. You're going to get to a business resolution somehow, so if you can avoid litigation and the associated time and money to do it, that's what you should do. But sometimes litigation can't be avoided.

How the Role of the Lawyer has Changed

What the entrepreneurs and managers want, and what the lawyers have to provide, is a very aggressive, proactive approach. This means that the effective lawyers are viewed by the company as quasi-members of the management team, whose particular expertise is law - like the expertise of the company's CFO is finance or accounting. The effective lawyers are the ones who are brought in early on by the entrepreneurs on any matter that has any potential legal ramifications. Sometimes those lawyers are brought in on non-legal issues because they have excellent business and financial judgment and the experience to provide counsel to a company.

Carl A. Cohen is the co-chairman of Buchanan Ingersoll's Technology and Entrepreneurial Services Group. In a recent profile of Carl, the Pittsburgh Business Times said, "If there is indeed an art to deal making, Carl Cohen seems to have mastered it." Carl has extensive experience in venture capital, public offerings, mergers and acquisitions, corporate partnering, and other financial transactions. He also functions as general counsel for growing companies, playing a key role in business decisions which have legal implications and helping manage legal matters.

MARK A. FISCHER

The Copyright Revolution

Palmer & Dodge LLP

Co-Chairperson of Publishing & Entertainment Group, Internet/E-Commerce Group, and Intellectual Property Group

Background

When I left law school, I set up my solo practice in Harvard Square. I started in entertainment law representing rock bands, musicians, and authors. From there, I joined a small firm consisting of six attorneys. I then headed to an intellectual property firm where I worked for about 10 years before joining Palmer & Dodge five years ago. The practice has always centered on creativity: working with creative people and creative companies. This meant at the outset that I was working with musicians and authors; later book publishers and software companies. Today, perhaps half of my practice involves Internet-related companies and the other half involves entertainment, interactive developers, film, television, publishers, record companies and intellectual property matters. These clients are highly creative people, as is very much the case with the universities with which I work.

Interesting Aspects

The first and most important unifying factor is what I really love most about what I do: the connections between otherwise seemingly different people. It's an exceptionally diverse group of people. But the connection is that so many people I represent have the compulsion to create one way or another and they would do so regardless of the circumstances. For example, most musicians will create music whether it's in a garage or in a basement, whether they get paid or not. Now many of them want to be superstars and they want to be wildly paid and get all the benefits of fame, but they do it anyway. This enthusiasm and commitment cuts across all forms of creativity. They care very passionately about what they do and a lot of them are personally offended by some of the issues involved in some of the technologies that use (without permission) what they've worked so very hard and so well to create.

One of new factors is how creative people may have to be renaissance men and women. It used to be that if you were a good composer, singer, songwriter, you'd find somebody to record you and you might find some people to help promote you. I was on a panel at Harvard University with Chuck D, the rapper, who used to be with Public Enemy, and he is a renaissance man. He knows the technology and he knows the Internet, so he's a technologist. He knows how to promote himself and he's a musician. He has to have all these characteristics. The most challenging issue today is how musicians have to know so much more. Instead of a thousand great ideas for a creator in most areas of creativity (not just musicians), creators may now have to know ten thousand things. They have to know how the Internet works, for example. Could Mozart have done everything that we expect Chuck D to do to be a professional musician?

When I used to teach at Berklee College of Music, the question I asked the first day of the semester (when we usually had about 70 students) was "Why are you in this class?" One semester the first couple of students said something like "I want to learn more about the law and that's important to my career." The third student said, "I don't want to get ripped off!" And this was well before Napster. From then on, the next 67 or so said, "I don't want to get ripped off." I think a unifying factor for individual musicians, bands, and record companies is how the legal consciousness and the understanding of laws is now important to the greatest degree that I've ever seen in 20 years of law practice. People have to think about legal issues because each of us has the power to distribute in a way that only the biggest companies had years ago. A person with an Internet site can reach the whole world. You may have to spend a lot of money to get the world to look at you, but what an amazing ability we have to reach other. Everyone is a publisher and you know you can get to the penguins in Antarctica. You can get to almost anybody with an Internet connection, and that's an incredible power. So legal issues are for everyone now, from the biggest Internet company to the loneliest musician.

Biggest Developments With Respect to Internet Law

The biggest development is that everyone has fantastic questions, and the answers are really up in the air. The questions are just everywhere and everyone is looking at things in new ways. The traditional content industries of music, motion pictures, and publishing are truly being viewed in a brand new way in terms of new systems of distributing and new ways of paying for it (or in some cases, not paying for it). For the first time many people, especially consumers, are learning what copyright law is and they are questioning the whole premise of copyright. So from a copyright perspective these are the most fascinating of times as the whole framework of copyright is being challenged. Many people think the traditional system of rewarding creativity by providing incentives to create may not be as important as consumption. I don't share that view because I think we have to balance allowing consumers to have access to content with the obvious fact that creators deserve to be paid. Taking Napster as an example because it is in the news these days, while Napster is wondrous, cool technology, why should musicians have to give their work up for free just because consumers want it free? While Napster is a very cool toy it should be linked to payment to the creators. To me that's only common sense and only fair. Technology has always led the copyright law. It is very true today. Because most of my practice is transactional (making deals happen and also acting as an agent), we are seeing the nature of contracts change.

Important Precedents

In the course of one year, the biggest, hottest, sexiest, most interesting question is Napster, a question we didn't have a year ago. We don't know in the next year or two or three which technologies the content industries will develop to try to fight back, and we don't know what the business models will be. I'm optimistic that content owners will do well, ultimately. They have tremendous economic power and resources. My best guess is that we're going to see a mild revolution in copyright law. But we will not entirely know when or where we're going to settle until some of the Internet-based technologies are resolved. In other words the technology is still evolving so rapidly that the law can't possibly catch up instantly. I don't think we're going to have the answers applicable to the next fifty years just within the next year or two. We are undergoing a truly radical, dramatic transformation on how people receive content. But, copyright laws did really well when dealing with issues surrounding making a physical copy. These laws don't address so adeptly issues regarding transmission and the new values of access, timeliness, and value-added services.

Biggest Legal Issues Companies Face

A very large number of cases involve cybersquatters of domain names. I represent CMGI and its network of companies. On behalf of AltaVista, a company largely owned by CMGI, our firm has won numerous domain name squatter cases and certainly cybersquatting is a major issue for many companies, particularly Internet-based companies. Another area is the interplay between content and technology like Napster. Many of my clients are either content companies trying to figure out how to work with the new technology; others are companies that don't have much content who are trying to figure out what the law allows them to do with regard to other people's content. To a certain extent these technological systems rely upon the "kindness of strangers," and, therefore, a significant concern is trying to figure out where copyright law is headed so technology-based companies can build technology structures and use other people's content in ways that are likely to be compatible with developments in the law in the future. That task is very difficult in relation to the new technical laws like the Digital Millennium Copyright Act and the Audio Home Recording Act.

Important Matters

I represent some large universities and one of the big issues for them is distance education on the Internet and other forms of transmission as they try to understand the rules of this new road. Faculty members who historically owned their own course work and course packs were able to keep all rights of publication. On the other hand, copyright law suggests that the universities own those course materials under the work made-for-hire doctrine. In distance education endeavors, many of the colleges and universities in this country believe they're providing much greater resources and are making a far greater contribution to faculty members' work than with respect to "traditional" teaching. Furthermore, many colleges and universities are creating subsidiaries, profit or non-profit, to work in the distance education realm. One of the most important questions is whether faculty members own the content that universities present through distance education or whether the universities or their subsidiaries own them. In the employment arena this is very important because intellectual property is clearly at the core. And should a faculty member be exclusive to one university? May he or she simultaneously participate in another school's or another company's distance education system, too. These are very significant employment issues.

Important Clauses to Include in Copyright Contracts

The most important thing is trying to work out the future of distribution rights so that rights are appropriately apportioned between the licensor and the licensee, making sure the economics of the contract work now and during the duration of the contract.

For example, let's say you're an independent author. If you're dealing as an individual author with a publisher, you might tell the publisher that the typical royalty for a hard cover book or a trade book (as opposed to a professional book) is 10% for the first 5,000 copies at retail, 12½ % for the next 5,000, 15% for subsequent copies and professional publishing royalties are somewhere around 2/3rds of those rates. As the author, you tell the publisher that you want the customary rates and that you understand the publisher has to print, bind, and distribute the book. There are returns of books from the bookstores as well to take into account. But, the economics of "e-publishing" may be very different than from traditional books. The publisher may decide to distribute your book online. If you have an e-book that is downloaded to the Palm Pilot of the future (one that's easy to read - we haven't gotten there yet, however), should the author get 15% after 10,000 copies or should the author get 50% in a paperless book? I strongly believe the revenue will be there for both publishers and authors, but maybe it should be apportioned differently than it is today. So, how do you deal as an author and a publisher with a book contract when the fundamental rules existing more or less since Gutenberg (or at least since the development of the mass market paperback) are now shifting?

Partnerships

In theory almost everybody likes to partner. It's my experience, however, that many partnerships in the truest sense don't work. Partnerships of different companies are very hard to implement because often they lack the motivation. Perhaps, in the broadest sense, a license is a partnership in that someone is supplying something that it does well to another party, which might be a distributor or licensee contributing what it does well. The first point to look at is to make sure the roles are well defined and each of the two partners is doing what it does best. You don't want people put in a position where they are doing something far away from their core mission and their core competency. Partnerships where one party or both parties are not clear about their particular roles or where one party is put into the position of doing something that it's not particularly strong at, are unlikely to succeed. Another thing to look out for is just how fast it all moves. One of the challenges for people who try to partner and have some kind of collaboration is that competitive and technological environments change so quickly. The other factors are probably obvious to you. Who controls what? If the parties don't agree, what happens?

Smartest Legal Moves

Very small startup companies need to make sure that they have something proprietary, particularly intellectual property. They need to make sure that they have names that are clear, that they're not going to build goodwill with a name only to find out that someone else has rights to that trademark. They should search the trademarks and protect them vigorously. One of the mistakes that small companies make is they don't do a little bit of work searching internationally in Europe, Japan, Brazil, and other countries with significant markets. They should make sure their name is viable in other countries and sensitive to local culture and local languages because the Internet is inherently international.

Some small companies make the mistake of not thinking big. They have to plan as if they're going to succeed so that they don't give away equity to the pizza delivery folk because they deliver the pizza on time. They should also certainly, like movie producers, avoid giving away more than 100% of the equity. Small companies have a strange disconnect at times, both undervaluing and overvaluing themselves. What I mean by that is sometimes they believe they're going to be big and think as big as all outdoors and at other times they think so very small and start giving away equity, which really compromises the future when they really do need to undertake additional rounds of funding. The founders will then lose control far earlier than they should and while they value their future, they somehow don't value themselves sufficiently. Now for bigger companies it's a very different matter because the Internet has developed a base of very bright, experienced people who have developed enormous experience on an incredibly fast track and with incredible intensity. They have absorbed and learned so much so quickly and there's a phenomenal energy. There, I think, the mistakes are rarely legal; the mistakes are more business-related. I think the legal interplay arises with people who may have so much to do in so short a time that they enter into agreements that conflict with other agreements or don't allow the flexibility to get out of transactions.

The Importance of Confidentiality Agreements

Confidentiality Agreements are not as important as some people think. So many factors go into success. There are numerous e-commerce companies. For example, Amazon.com sells books and Barnes & Noble sells books. The idea of each business, in a broad sense, of selling books is not proprietary or exclusive. Yet so many people think that the idea by itself is so much more important than the quality of the business plan, the importance of the managers, and the quality and quantity of the money. There are so many other factors relating to success that, in my view, while confidentiality agreements are important, they are overrated. Such confidentiality agreements are helpful in a defensive kind of way. By and large, most responsible business people will honor confidentiality even if there wasn't an agreement. In the book industry, for example, rarely are there confidentiality agreements when an author provides a manuscript to a prospective publisher. Most responsible publishers know that the idea of the book is not as important as how it's written, who the author is, how it's distributed, and how it's promoted. However, confidentiality agreements often do have value when it comes to technical information that can't be protected by patents, for example.

Privacy Issues

There's all this talk about personal information and keeping it private with regard to click stream data and so forth, which is hugely important. But one of the hidden issues is corporate data and corporate information because in a business-to-business world, if you're ordering 100,000 of the proverbial widgets, the company that has that data knows something about your business and they might have a competitive advantage. That's a good time for a confidentiality agreement to provide defensive protection. Corporate privacy to me is one of the large future issues, because in a business-to-business world, companies will be making significant disclosures by what they're ordering online. Although this risk existed in traditional purchasing situations, the ability of suppliers to instantaneously aggregate data and identify patterns has been greatly enhanced by online systems. In the personal privacy arena, certainly, you will see increasing privacy regulation, in addition to the regulation that already exists with regard to children. The concept of privacy law may have been created in Cambridge and Boston, in a Harvard Law Review article by Louis Brandeis and Samuel Warren. Warren was apparently outraged by gossip columns of the day that mentioned his wife, who was active socially. So that article had humble and intrinsically personal beginnings.

One mistake companies make is they have privacy policies that are really good, but they don't follow them. We conduct many Web site audits for companies and we find that many companies have really well-crafted policies, but there's no connection between the lawyer somewhere in an office who's written this really elegant little policy and the business people who haven't even read it.

Another thing about privacy that's fascinating is there's not always a common agreement as to what privacy should be. For example, I do a lot of work in print and online medical publishing. If you use a medical Web site and you have a family member with an illness, you may welcome the fact that the Web site knows what medication your family member takes for that condition. You may welcome an email telling you there's been a product recall. You may be thankful that there's this Web site that may help save the life or improve the health of someone in your family. On the other hand, the family member may not want someone to know he or she is taking this medicine for a particular condition. You may not want a connection between the drugstore and your prescriptions from this Web site. So one of the big questions about privacy is that some people consider certain things private and they're absolutely right, and other people don't care and they're absolutely right, too, because privacy is subjective. Reasonable people have different views. I think the future of privacy law is "opting in" - requiring an affirmative consumer act to receive emails and other targeted material, in contrast to requiring the consumer to "opt out" after the fact. In other words, we will see more and more places for consumers and businesses to be asked to determine what flavors and what degrees of privacy they want.

What to Look for in a Web Site Audit

The first thing is to make sure that a Web site has a privacy policy, to make sure the site has the right intellectual property notices, and to make sure that if it's an e-commerce site that it has the appropriate click-through agreements dealing with warranties, returns, refunds, and taxes. If there is content that appears to be from another source, it must be properly licensed. The new e-signature laws will help us enormously in contract formation. Publicly-traded companies have SEC compliance issues in Web sites contract. Some Web sites have a safe harbor from copyright liability, but may need to comply with the requirement for appointment of an agent under the DMCA. Those are some of the things you look for.

Developing Legal Issues

There is encryption, but as we've seen in the news, the codes have a tendency to be cracked. That is an important privacy issue because it is unlikely that wireless signals are going to be as safe as wires. The issue also comes from the fact that so much consumer activity and behavior will be conducted through the device. If you have this little mobile device that you will order your groceries from and make your dinner reservations with, then whatever phone company or wireless company with whom you're dealing will have access to pretty much your whole life. When it gets to the point where the company will know exactly where you are and what street you're walking down, and this little device has your browser, date book, and all of your personal contacts - the picture becomes clear. Some of this data will be on some central server. The U.S. is way, way behind in m-commerce. If you've been to Japan or Europe, people in those areas are using these devices much more so than those in the U.S.

It is pretty much the belief that the U.S. is much more experienced in Internet-related litigation because we helped create the Internet. Also, perhaps perversely, we are the leaders in litigation in the world. There is no question that the rest of the world looked to us with regard to jurisdiction issues, such as determining where and how to resolve a dispute among different states and different countries. But because we are beginning to lag in m-commerce and the Europeans have moved ahead on privacy data protection, we are not always the leaders. The European data privacy directive was a critical event and the U.S. tried to work out our different views with other countries, which we seem to have done now.

In the content world, if you are part of a multi-national company that has employees or reporters around the world, what happens if it publishes an article that someone in a Muslim country believes is blasphemy? There are two high profile cases in this general area in the last few years. One involved a CompuServe employee arrested in Germany and convicted for charges involving child pornography that appeared on CompuServe through absolutely no fault or knowledge on the part of the employee. The conviction was overturned ultimately. Just a couple of months ago in France, Yahoo (through its U.S. site) was auctioning Nazi-related memorabilia and there was an action brought against Yahoo with regard to activity that is not illegal in the U.S. but might be illegal in France. Further, it's much easier to be found libelous in the UK than it is here in the U.S. So, will contracts have to be written to deal with the most restrictive country in regard to defamation, blasphemy and censorship? Will Web site contracts be "dumbed down" to be consistent with the most restrictive laws in the world?

Another example concerns warranty protection. The U.S., being the home of capitalism in its active form, allows more waiving of warranties than other countries like Australia. We need to provide provisions in Internet e-commerce contracts that say that if the contracting party is a German company, German law may apply, but if you're in Australia, Australian law may apply. That may be the future of contracts - for a while.

Developments on the Horizon

We will see a short-term resolution of the laws on file sharing and file swapping. The technology will continue to develop. Enforcement will continue to be extremely difficult, but we will hear the courts speak. On a strictly legal front, I expect content owners to continue to do well within the courtrooms. But whether or not the legal system will be able to deal with real world use is the harder question. The implications of this trend are that content owners will have to look for non-legal business solutions to be of greater assistance than the law alone. The law alone on the content side will not be enough. Second, you will see changes in the copyright law itself. Copyright laws will change to deal with issues of access and transmission to a much greater degree, and in that respect, copyright law will become far more intricate and far more elaborate. The copyright laws will begin to resemble the Internal Revenue Code and deal with more idiosyncratic situations in more excruciating detail. Next, on privacy, there is strong public support for greater privacy protection and you will see more thorough laws requiring "opt-in" for consumers to get email and for their data to be shared.

Becoming a Leader

I would say the one thing that's important for leaders to understand is that virtually every decision affects more people than one would think at first glance. Most business decisions impact many different people and many different communities. Good leaders care about the people with whom, and for whom, they work. Ironically, the Internet increases connections, in time and geography, yet we are often more physically disconnected. One characteristic of a good leader is having enough information to make the right decision despite the distractions.

Mark A. Fischer is a partner at Palmer & Dodge LLP in Boston. He represents creative companies, institutions, and individuals in new media, entertainment, publishing, trademark, and computer law. His practice emphasizes the laws and business of music, motion pictures, electronic commerce, and new media endeavors, including the Internet and DVDs, that link entertainment and information with technology. His clients include CMGI, Inc. and its network of companies, Hasbro Interactive, and Rounder Records.

Mark is Co-Chairperson of the Palmer & Dodge Publishing and Entertainment Group, the Internet/E-Commerce Group, and the firm's Intellectual Property Group. He is also Chairperson of Palmer & Dodge's in-house Technology Committee overseeing the acquisition, development, and use of technology within the firm. A frequent lecturer and author, he has taught Entertainment Law and Intellectual Property courses at Berklee College of Music, Boston College Law School, Northeastern University School of Law, New England School of Law, and Massachusetts Continuing Legal Education ("MCLE"). He currently teaches the Advanced Copyright course at Suffolk University Law School. He co-chairs the World Law Group's Intellectual Property/Internet Practice Group.

BRIAN VANDENBERG

Privacy Rights and Ownership of Content

uBid.com

General Counsel/VP Corporate Development

Background

My background is primarily in commercial transactional law, although I exclusively litigated for a short time following law school. After five years with a mid-sized Chicago firm, I formed my own firm with a number of colleagues. During this time, I represented a company that was headed by our current CEO, so he and I have had a professional relationship for quite a few years. When uBid was looking for in-house general counsel, I was also looking for a change. An in-house role was really what made sense for me, so we worked something out and I came aboard.

Most Exciting Part of Being Corporate Counsel for an Internet Company

I'm attracted to the challenge of growing a business and contributing to a long-term business objective rather than representing a host of clients on a project basis. My role here is beyond that of just general counsel. I'm actively involved in management, business development and other areas of our business.

Most Important Issues

The Internet space is evolving and changing rapidly in many ways. In particular, a key is ensuring that we understand not only the legalities impacting our business but also the social preferences and expectations in areas like privacy and permission marketing. Specifically, understanding when people want to hear from us, and making sure that we're striking that fine balance between being available and being intrusive. The Internet uniquely positions us to do that, but at the same time, we don't want to be in our customer's face. That's sometimes a difficult line to walk and we want to maintain a good relationship with our customers.

Major Legal Issues That Internet Companies are Facing

Privacy is one, and we're very respectful of it, so I don't see that as much of an issue. I think it's clear how to handle that.

One of the unique challenges for an e-commerce firm is dealing with the legal issues that relate to the nature of our contract with the customer, if there is one. For example, is an order on the Internet an enforceable contract? Is the answer different in auction versus a fixed-price environment? In auctions, what are the parties' legal rights and responsibilities if a unique item is damaged, and substitutes are not available? The analogy is like this: if a newspaper advertisement for a brick and mortar retailer promotes the availability of a product, but does not have the product when I arrive to purchase it, do I have a legal claim to say, "Your newspaper advertisement was an offer, and I've accepted that offer?" The Internet provides unique challenges in regards to quantities available. Another question might be, "What are the legal rights and responsibilities in the event of error in a product description?" And independent of the legal issue might be, "How do we satisfy the customer from a pure business standpoint, irrespective of what the legal obligations are?" It's another fine line.

Advantages to Having In-House General Counsel

It's an invaluable resource, particularly for a company that's grown at the speed at which we've grown and has the transactional volume we have. The pace at which we operate daily is incredible. We're active in numerous marketing and other partnerships, and implement new deals quickly. Having to forward our day-to-day legal work to outside counsel isn't realistic and would be a competitive disadvantage, because the Internet space moves so quickly. If we were unable to immediately implement decisions impacting our site, waiting for outside counsel, we'd be losing. The results of what we're doing on the site are immediately measurable in traffic and other quantifiable metrics, unlike traditional marketing. Therefore, when a decision is made, it's implemented immediately. The Internet really commands that pace.

What to Protect Your Company From in Business Development Deals

One is ownership of data. If we're in a partnership, joint venture or a co-branding relationship, we need to ensure that the sensitive customer data that is collected is being protected. It's important to ensure that the information is treated confidentially and in a way that respects the privacy of the customer.

Another is flexibility. This goes back to how quickly the industry changes. We are careful to build in appropriate provisions that give us flexibility. Sometimes that's simply termination rights for convenience, irrespective of whether there's been a failure to perform by either party. A relationship and a deal structure that's great today conceivably could be a horrendous deal for us six months from now, because of the speed at which the Internet has evolved and changed. An example is the marketing shift from impressions-based marketing deals to performance-based marketing deals. We won't do an impressions-based deal today and a year ago, we would have. So much is changing so quickly.

Wearing Many Hats

Most of the in-house lawyers at Internet companies that I know and deal with do wear many hats. They're not just doing legal work and many are involved in business development and other management roles. My role includes business development activities, and also extends to some involvement, in some cases informal, in most of the areas of our business.

Important Issues of the Future

Bottom line profitability, or at least a legitimate plan to get to profitability. Until recently, the industry's focus had been on revenue growth, with a tolerant expectation that Internet companies would bleed red ink for some period of time. There's certainly less tolerance for that now. My role is to assist in structuring deals with our financial goals in mind, ensuring that they're structured with bottom line earnings in mind, as opposed to simply helping drive revenue on the top line.

Other Issues That will Come to a Head in the Next Year

One that is a bit unique to auctions, but I think is relevant elsewhere and will come to a head, is that of content ownership. The context I'm referring to is, for example, the ongoing dispute between eBay and Bitters Edge. Does eBay have some proprietary rights to the listings that its users post on its site, and what legal rights does it have from preventing firms like a Bitters Edge from spidering and pulling that content and redistributing it in a search function?

We'll see more law coming in on the enforceability of on-line agreements, when a customer or user goes to a site clicks an "I accept" button in order to use the site. Is that truly an enforceable contract? Is it arm's length? There's very little law that speaks to this issue, or one or two cases that guide us in some respects, and it's still an open question as to how that works. I suspect that the question will hinge on subtleties like the positioning of a user agreement in the registration process.

We'll also continue to see more on the relationship between domain names and traditional trademark law. I can't tell you the number of clear domain knockoffs that come across my desk almost every day. In an auction format, people take a variation of uBid.com and put some other word in it or a number next to it, still carrying out our color schemes and fonts, trying to spin themselves or take advantage of whatever goodwill we've created.

Another area still evolving is patents. A case in point is Amazon and the patent for its one-click ordering system. What is patentable technology? And is the traditional patent protection period still appropriate? Should there be some revision of patent law in general because of the uniqueness of technology and the Internet? These are questions that will all need to be answered.

Biggest Mistakes Being Made

Poor communication, generally. In particular, I often see inappropriate and unenforceable disclaimers with respect to services or products. In some cases, the language is effective, but it's inconspicuous on the site. It's especially challenging with the Internet, because you can't control when and where a user's going to click.

International Issues

Part of it is the domain name issue. If a company wishes to do business internationally, there will likely be an interest in carrying its brand internationally, including owning the top-level domain name country by country. In some cases, these domain names may be registered by third-parties, including squatters. Anti-squatting legislation varies country by country, making it necessary in some cases to negotiate to acquire the domain name. However, there's increasing legal clarity on this issue; United Nations Arbitration Court has recently come down with some favorable rulings, requiring squatters to give up domain names.

With e-commerce in particular, issues involving customs laws, currencies and language translation are relevant. Translation is interesting because it impacts the nature and accuracy of product descriptions, representations and warranties. Sites are increasingly looking to robust translation software to assist in global growth, yet most software is unable to translate with complete accuracy. It highlights the potential legal implications of advancing technology.

Finally, Internet use internationally is lagging behind the U.S. The size of the wired audience alone presents challenges in developing a viable international strategy. Of course, the audience will grow quickly, as it has in the States.

Advice for Internet Startups

From a legal standpoint, I would recommend a comprehensive and conspicuous user agreement, clearly setting forth the terms and conditions of visitors use of the site.

I'm also a privacy advocate. I harp on this one, and am probably a broken record. If the privacy of customers and users is not respected through well-established and embraced policies, you'll fail.

Additionally, there needs to be sensitivity to Internet fraud concerns. Make sure that you've got proper legal structure in place and proper representations, warranties, and disclaimers. Again, it comes down to communication. Are you the seller of products, with warranty obligations and similar responsibilities, or are you merely a forum or community in which third users transact business with one another? There also needs to be familiarity and compliance with FTC rules and regulations that uniquely apply to Internet transactions.

From a general business standpoint, make sure that the business model itself is sustainable. In the beginning, anything that had a .com by it got funded irrespective of whether the business model was viable. Be your own worst critic. Have a solid business plan and put a strong management team in place to execute on it. A path to profitability is critical.

MARK I. GRUHIN

Business Intelligence From Day One

Schmeltzer, Aptaker & Shepard, P.C.

Partner

Background

I've been practicing law for about 20 years. I've also done some investment banking and have been involved in some exciting startups. I consider myself a business lawyer, more than necessarily an Internet or biotech lawyer. Nevertheless, I do a lot of work with Internet business, as well as biotechnology businesses, primarily assisting them with their growth and attraction of capital. I have represented both the startup company, as well as the investor. I generally act as counsel for companies throughout their growth period. I assist these companies in many facets, from corporate documentation to contractual negotiation and business planning.

Major Trends

There are a lot of dynamic changes happening. The excitement surrounding the Internet and the biotech market has invigorated a lot of experienced people, many who have grown up in larger companies, to reach out and start their own companies. In addition, younger generations of entrepreneurs have begun to start their own ventures.

Dynamic changes have begun in the capital markets. In the beginning of the "Internet Rush," venture capitalists were chasing dot.coms. Unfortunately many got burned. Now venture capitalists are primarily investing in infrastructure and telecom. While there remains some money chasing the startup deal, I do think the money's getting more conservative as the economy and the markets begin to change.

The Beginning of a Relationship With a New Company

What distinguishes me from other lawyers is that I am a businessman in addition to being a lawyer, which enables me to understand the business transaction that my clients are considering or desire to achieve. I have to decide when it is prudent to enter into a contract or to raise capital. It is difficult to advise my clients without being familiar with the fundamentals of their business, or without understanding the business relationships that they seek. If you are familiar with your client's business, you will have better success advising them on the kinds of legal risks they choose to face. There are a lot of lawyers who will approach deals without understanding the business terms. Most of my clients come to me because I offer both legal and business skills. I tend to help them negotiate transactions, not simply to document them. Often, I am the actual negotiator on behalf of companies, almost the way an inside business development person might act. I will often step in and not only advise, but also take the lead depending upon their needs.

Biggest Mistakes Being Made

There are a few major things. First, many startups naively believe that they are going to easily raise capital because they have a good idea. However, they need to understand the people from whom they are seeking capital. Just because a venture firm or an institutional firm or even an angel has money, doesn't mean that their company is the appropriate investment for them. Secondly, they really need to road test their business plans. Startups should find professionals in law, finance and in their industry and have these professionals challenge their business plan before they seek money. I think that entrepreneurs are so excited about getting a business started that they do not test their plans enough and they go to the capital markets too soon. There is a very strong fraternity among venture firms because they all participate in deals. It's not one against the other and when you go to one venture firm and they don't like the deal, you'll often find that the message has been conveyed to other people in the marketplace. I think it's very important that an entrepreneur understands where he's seeking money, understands the people he's planning to get in bed with, and finds the right professionals to help him.

Most Common Problems for Internet Companies

As companies grow and expand their internal services, they improve their ability to oversee and mitigate mistakes, whether it's in human resources or intellectual property. Larger companies tend to be aware of those issues but it's a process. Since many of the high-tech companies are young and possess an environment of openness, they don't bring the kind of discipline that is found in traditional companies. Therefore, they can face issues that are plaguing the rest of society, like sexual harassment, and perhaps be less prepared to address those problems; but I think that these startups learn quickly as they evolve.

Business Development Agreements

Companies should always look at deals and make business judgments first. Obviously, they need to cut the best deals possible. They need to make sure that they're in bed with people who understand their business and who are trying to be fair with the business terms as well. Startups for example, like any other business, need to be prudent when entering into a contract and need to understand each party's responsibilities during the life of a contract. They need to make sure that the contract appropriately reflects the deal they made and that there are appropriate protections to allow either side to exit the contract while simultaneously protecting each other's intellectual property rights and other benefits. They need to carefully consider their overall contractual relationship, the impact on their revenue model, and the tax implications as well.

Employee Issues

I think it's very important that companies work with professionals who can provide them with the appropriate types of documents to protect a whole host of things early in their development. These protections might include non-disclosure of confidential information, enforcement provisions, protections of intellectual property, and anti-solicitation of employees if people are going to leave. Employee handbooks, sexual harassment policies, email policies, and Internet guidelines are just a few of the policies that will help defend a company from future lawsuits as well as to give them the ability to enforce their rights against the people with whom they are involved.

Capital Formation Issues

There is often a lot of confusion about incentive stock options, non-statutory incentive stock options, restricted stock agreements and the tax implications of these and other choices. It seems that everyone wants to create ISO's, not necessarily because they're best for the business, since it depends on the type of business that one is in, but because these are tools needed to attract good employees, whether or not there might be other alternatives. From a tax perspective, there is a distinction between ISO's and non-qualified options. However, little emphasis has been placed on the alternative minimum tax implications to employees so they really don't understand that ISO's aren't necessarily as good as they might seem. In terms of capitalization and the employment arena, you often see distinctions between preferred stock and common stock according to a valuation. This is done primarily to recognize the difference between how a company requires a financier to evaluate a company versus how a company needs to value itself in order to attract employees of quality. Ultimately, those two valuations need to merge. Sometimes problems occur when valuations are too high and market changes create "down rounds." These events can accelerate the loss of a high tech startup company's most valuable possession, its human resources. Other problems sometimes occur with regard to the chemistry between the representatives of the investors and the founders of a company. Expectations need to be clear from the beginning in order to avoid meltdown of management.

The Right Time for Companies to Get In-House Counsel

It depends upon the sophistication of the business and its budget. I work with companies that are very large from a revenue standpoint, but don't necessarily need in-house counsel. I also work with companies that haven't quite achieved significant revenues or are pre-revenue companies that have in-house counsel. It's a cost analysis formula. It varies from business to business; it's just a matter of cost. Often you'll find that companies prefer to deal with outside counsel as they grow in early formation. As they grow to become more mature companies, they tend to figure out that there may be certain legal functions that they can do in-house more cheaply or have greater control internally.

Major Issues From a Legal Standpoint

Lawyers have recently become more focused on advising clients about privacy issues and the Internet as those issues rise to the forefront. Regarding biotech, there are a lot of intellectual property issues raised in terms of gene discovery and how the patent office will recognize it. I think that as our industries change, new issues arise that are not necessarily different in terms of theoretical legal concepts. However, their platform might be different, so issues that might face an Internet company are distinct simply because they're on the Web. There may be greater focus on those as an industry as a whole, but that doesn't mean that if you're not on the Web that you don't have those kinds of issues.

Online Privacy Issues

A lot of current controversial issues have to do with disclosure. Just like you're obligated to provide financial disclosures to your investors and your customers, you are also obligated to disclose your privacy policies. I think there was a misconception among the average consumer that when they got on the Internet it was private and that they couldn't be traced as to what they were doing. This reaction was based upon lack of understanding about the medium's function. As people begin to understand more about "cookies," for example, and how Internet companies might generate revenue by selling information about them they become more focused on the privacy issue. There's money in information and it allows advertisers and others to be more direct in what they're selling an individual whether or not the individual is inclined to share that information. As the consumer becomes more aware of what the marketplace is and what companies are doing, they will become more sensitive to the issue and will demand appropriate disclosures and safeguards. There have been companies that have promised privacy and then have breached those promises and been faced with investigations from the government. My suggestion is "buyer beware" until there is greater uniformity on the Internet.

Landmark Cases

Well, imagine that the Internet is a sort of spectrum. One side of the spectrum has a wild, wild west aspect and it's promoting a tremendous economic growth and helping to drive our economy to its current state: tremendously accessible and instantaneous information. That side is exciting, but as it succeeds there are consequences to its success. For example, states are thinking that they are going to start losing revenue because they can't apply sales tax. This issue is what's driving the tax arguments and I suspect that ultimately there will be a slow evolution of a plan that will be fair to the states. It is the same situation as to the privacy issue: a balancing act between privacy rights and first amendment rights while simultaneously promoting the sharing of information to generate commerce and the exchange of ideas. Unfortunately, just like anything in a free society, this balance can be abused and as time goes on our society will evolve ways to determine what is tolerable and intolerable. In the same way that we have regulated television, society will eventually regulate the Internet as well. There is a strong constituency to preclude that from happening and I think that it is a matter of evolution and where our country might be in terms of its political sense at any one time. Whether moderate, conservative, or reform, I think that is what's going to help dictate and control our technologies as they expand.

Biggest Legal Issues in the Future

I don't think there's any one issue. I think that it's safe to say that young companies want to be part of the 21st century technology, are looking to grow, and are facing the same kinds of problems that all companies face as they grow. I think they need counsel with regard to the basic types of legal requirements, like corporate governesses and dealing with human resources, as well as assistance with more cutting edge issues of Internet privacy, intellectual property protection, strategic partnering and those kinds of legal issues that are evolving as our industries change. I do think that the period of dot.com downfall has served as a wake up call to entrepreneurs that simply advancing to the Internet for the sake of being there is not going to stand the test of time. They are realizing that they have to be real businesses with real profits coming in the near future, and that they will have to give greater scrutiny to their business models and plans and the legal and financial issues surrounding them.

Issues That Will Haunt Failing Dot.com Companies

There are a lot of companies that felt such tremendous pressure to go to the street early even though they were so young. This is a dynamic change. When a company goes public, it faces two primary things that are different than when a company is a private company. One is regulatory requirements that it must meet quarter after quarter. The next is meeting the expectations of financial analysts quarter after quarter. If you miss your plan by a few pennies you can just crash and burn. Unfortunately I think a lot of young companies didn't have sound business or financial plans in the first place and didn't spend enough time privately, out of the public eye to test their models. Now these companies are going to be faced with greater investor scrutiny and potentially, lawsuits.

The Protection of Intellectual Property

I think that most companies approach their intellectual property prudently and they seek out professional advice. However, the most important thing to a lot of these companies is human resources, meaning those people who know how to build the company and grab market share. It is important for these companies to grab as much of the market even if there is a lot of competition in the marketplace. I think there are a lot of companies that were able to raise huge sums of money not because they had such an exclusive idea but because they believed and were able to convince others that they could and had the experience to grab a huge market share.

The Importance of Confidentiality Agreements

I think they are important, but oftentimes they tend to be so broad that courts narrow them or find them unenforceable. They need to be well written, specific in their terms, and have some teeth in terms of enforceability. Unfortunately the bigger problem is a balance of power. Often you will have a young company requiring a larger company to sign a confidentiality agreement, but ill-equipped to do anything about a breach because of lack of funds or lack of appropriate oversight.

I think the advice that I try to provide is that a company should not proceed based upon the belief that the confidentiality agreement will protect them the most. The thing that will protect them the most is being prudent in their business judgment. Companies must ask themselves who did they get involved with, how did they share information and how did they proceed in a way to mitigate the possibilities of being sued or having to sue someone.

Challenges of Doing Business Internationally

There are the issues regarding enforceability. Often my contract provisions will require that U.S. law apply, and if we are unable to accomplish that task, we generally seek arbitration in an E.C. country. If you're dealing with a third world country, however, or others where you have to go into their court systems, it is more difficult to succeed. Knowing the jurisdictions and the court systems here in the U.S. certainly tends to help U.S. companies, but again, it's a balancing of power issue. If you are negotiating with larger companies in Europe they tend to take a national approach as much as a U.S. company might.

Advice for Internet Startups

I challenge my Internet companies in their business plan. I make them understand their plan. I make them view their competition and understand it. I make them do a lot of homework before we go out and seek capital. They have to be prepared. They have to understand themselves and how they will manage their idea. They have to know who is in the marketplace and how are they going to protect themselves from a change in the marketplace. They must also know how to convince someone to invest in their company. It is not simply coming up with an idea and running to the street, it is challenging that idea and fine-tuning it. Companies must seek professionals and other experts in their particular market to help provide advice on deciding whether or not they do have a viable plan. Just do your homework.

From a legal standpoint, we make sure that we try to protect the idea if need be. If the client is developing an Internet company, for example, we want to make sure that the copyright and trademark rights have been protected. We will assist the startup in addressing its corporate policy issues and we will make sure that it is prepared in terms of its human resources. We will assist the company in thinking about how it is going to structure the board or if it is going to have an advisory board. We will want to make sure that the appropriate financial infrastructure and accounting are in place. We want to make sure that the company has retained all the necessary professionals and that the company has attracted the right management. If the entrepreneur does not have the ability to manage properly we will recommend persons who have more experience. We will provide all legal and business support necessary to assist the startup company in achieving its goal.

Becoming a Leader

I think people need to have a vision, and a confidence in executing that vision. They must have the ability to communicate ideas without necessarily undermining the other side. The ability to negotiate and communicate depends on your position of bargaining power. You must understand that before you begin a process. You need to understand who your opponent is and what his or her objective is in order for you to succeed in your objective. So, vision, ability to communicate, ability to understand, and confidence to do it all are all aspects of a good leader.

Mark I. Gruhin is a partner in the law firm of Schmeltzer, Aptaker & Shepard, P.C., a Washington based law firm. Mr. Gruhin heads the firm's practice in business and finance and regularly provides advice to public corporations and private organizations alike in the Washington, D.C. metropolitan area and throughout the country in a wide range of business, securities and financial transactions. Mr. Gruhin has assisted businesses in their efforts to raise capital in the private markets and by "going public" and in satisfying their continuous obligations to provide information to the public under the requirements of the Exchange Act of 1934.

In addition to practicing law, Mr. Gruhin was a principal in the investment firm, RMI Investment Corporation, specializing in organizing investments in real estate and closely held corporations. This business background, coupled with his substantial legal experience in the areas of finance, syndication, securities regulations and real estate, provides Mr. Gruhin with additional insights to his client's business transactions.

Mr. Gruhin is a 1978 Phi Beta Kappa honors graduate of Rutgers College, Rutgers University and a 1981 magna cum laude law review graduate of the Washington College of Law, American University.

ARNOLD LEVINE

Legal Rules for Internet Companies

Proskauer Rose, LLP

Chair, iPractice Group

Background

At the outset, with Proskauer I did a variety of things - a three-year general internship, a lot of work on a variety of theoretical issues involving accountant's liability for a major accounting firm, several litigations and some general corporate work. My first major area of responsibility was working, over a period of 15 to 20 years, in the tax shelter business for clients who were raising money from high net worth individuals for the purpose of investing in transactions that generated large tax deductions. The relevance of that to my present legal work was that these were extremely creative, innovative, aggressive businessmen who were always looking to find new ways of doing things and were not involved in conventional cookie-cutter deals. They were always trying to beat the competition and find new opportunities in terms of structuring transactions, maximizing tax benefits, and aggressively marketing transactions so as to reach the largest number of investors, but doing so in a manner consistent with the legal requirements, particularly complex tax and securities laws.

While I was doing that, I was also keeping my hand in a number of corporate areas and engaging in various aspects of firm management. I've always been engaged in many different kinds of activities. During the period immediately preceding my involvement in the Internet area, I was doing a lot of work in leveraged buyout funds, M & A deals, financing acquisitions and setting up funds that would raise the money that would be invested in deals.

A couple of years ago it became apparent that the most effective way to take advantage of what was an emerging and exploding area, the Internet area and certain areas of related technology, was to focus on it, to commit resources to it, and to be open to new types of arrangements with clients that involve more financial exposure for the law firm, including taking stock in these new entities as well. We committed to doing that as a firm, and, coincidentally, at about the same time, we had enhanced our intellectual property capabilities. We brought in some very strong patent lawyers and some trademark and copyright lawyers. Having made an institutional decision about two years ago to focus on this Internet area and to be more aggressive in our client relations in this area, we also brought on board a few senior lawyers who had a tremendous amount of experience in the venture capital area with firms that were mainly venture capital shops and who had done a lot of IPO work in the e-commerce area. After we had strengthened ourselves, we then went after the business.

Exciting Aspects

I put the most exciting parts of my job in three categories. One is that instead of doing the same deal 20 times with modest changes, there's a lot of stuff that's happening that hasn't been done before or is being done in a different way, with people bringing a new mindset to business and legal issues. There are a number of types of agreements that people weren't doing before. In many situations, there is no relying on a standard form for a loan agreement or standard form for an acquisition agreement because clients are involved in transactions that people haven't done before. For example, a client is not sure where the technology is going to go, so you're fighting about licensing rights and what field of use to protect, without even knowing what the field of use will turn out to be. All of this is very exciting and requires a fair amount of creative thinking.

The second part that I find stimulating is that the lawyers are often functioning in a role that has much more business input than one would have in traditional transactions. Institutional clients have done the same transaction many, many times. They know what they want to do. They'll often do a letter of intent and move very far along in the transaction before they engage their lawyers, and then their lawyers will assist them to make sure they've focused on the important issues, often non-business issues, and the lawyers will document the matter that protects the interest they're obtaining and minimizing their risk while securing the greatest advantage. With many Internet and e-commerce clients, the founders of the company or the CEOs don't have as much personal breadth of experience in some of the work they're doing and they have only limited senior management, so they're relying on their lawyers more to be counselors and business advisers, and that's a dimension that is refreshing and interesting.

The third interesting part of this practice is the intensity with which many of the entrepreneurs focus on their businesses. This is their whole life, and it imposes on the lawyer a tremendous responsibility, a sense of urgency that is different from the sense of urgency you get in a normal deal. In any traditional deal, time is the enemy of the deal. Deals have a life cycle where you want to get them closed within as short a time frame as you can, consistent with doing the appropriate diligence and exercising the appropriate care, because as time goes on deals get stale and the risk of not closing increases. If you need to face and solve problem after problem, people get weary, so there is an urgency even in old economy traditional deals. But despite that pressure to get those deals done, the sense of personal commitment is not the same as it is with Internet entrepreneurs. They're living and breathing this stuff, and it is exciting to share that level of enthusiasm and energy.

Most Important Issues for Internet Companies

This is a funny answer coming from a lawyer, but the major problem experienced by new Internet and technology companies is getting adequate levels of qualified senior management. They've got to get COOs, CEOs, CTOs, CFOs, top marketing guys, and obtaining qualified executives in these areas is extremely difficult. I represent one company, a spectacular technology company with a phenomenal product that's been reviewed in the trade presses very favorably. It's a small company that has raised $30 million and it has software technology that could create a huge company. They don't have the breadth and depth of Compaq or Dell or IBM or Microsoft, so their ability to get into the marketplace without selling out to a big company is uncertain. They are struggling to hire the right marketing people for example. That is the type of problem that I see frequently. I have another company that's also in the technology area. They need a first rate CFO and a COO, and the hiring job is made more difficult because the CEO of this company is reluctant to let go of control.

In the first company that I was talking about, the CEO who put the company together was a technology genius, but he wasn't good at business and he wasn't maximizing opportunities. Instead of finding applications that would enable the company to go forward and build a sound revenue model, he had such a grandiose view of what he wanted to accomplish that he never would have had a revenue stream, and he never would have raised money. It would have been a disaster had he remained CEO, and finally he had to be replaced.

One of the most important legal issues is being able to raise money without giving up excessive control. The original owners have total control if they own all the voting stock or usually control enough voting stock to do what they want. As the venture capital investors come in they want board representation, which is appropriate, and they want veto rights with respect to many substantive issues, including raising new money, what the terms of raising the new money will be, and what the valuations will be. They often seek veto rights on mergers and acquisitions, loans and mortgages and other items as well.

In many cases where the company is in a desperate shape they will sometimes raise some money from investors by issuing debt on terms adverse to the company. These investors then have the chance to hold up new rounds of financing, because often times subsequent rounds of venture capital financing don't want to come in subordinate to the debt position. So you're now in a position where people who may have a relatively modest investment in the company have the ability to blackmail the company because of their debt position and the reluctance of new VC money to come in subordinate to the debt. I was talking to a client recently where there's about $6 million in debt. The company has some exceptional technology, and they're about to do another round of VC financing, typically for preferred stock, but the debt holder is holding them up. He wants to be paid off, and the new money is not happy to come in and have a significant portion of the new money go to pay off an old investor. They really don't want to be in a subordinate position. They feel they should be in a priority position. I have a few of those situations now.

Most Important Issues for Startups

It really depends on the type of company. To start out, you need to raise enough money to run your business, whatever the applicable period of time is, so you don't spend all of management's time raising money. When I was a young lawyer a long time ago, a client of mine was going into business and some financial adviser who was the head of an accounting firm offered the following advice, "Whatever you think you need, triple the amount and raise the larger amount, because otherwise you're going to spend the next 12 months just going out into the market to raise funds to run your business, and your business hasn't even evolved." So the first thing is to secure enough money to operate the business and do the other things you need to do in terms of marketing, technology and strategic relations. That often entails giving up more of the company than you want to give up. In satisfying the need to get enough money, you may be forced to give up control.

The second recommendation I would make is don't give up too much control. Don't put anybody in a position where they can determine your fate and preclude you from doing what you need to do or where they have a blackmail position. But the first principle, "raise enough money," and the second principle, "don't give up control," are in conflict with each other. In a similar vein, you need good advisers, and the good advisers don't come cheap. They want stock, they want options, and they want protection. So here you have a conflict: you need good advisers, you want their value. You also want the prestige that will add, even though that often is an overrated contribution. But you are reluctant to pay too much. As a result you'll often lock yourself into deals where if things go sour with the talent, as they often do, you may have people owning a meaningful piece of the company who haven't made a meaningful contribution. That's another balancing act. If it were simple there would be no problems, but the fact is that often there are competing needs, and because of that competing need you can't protect all the interests you'd like to protect.

Another area of significance to me is the technology area. Often you want to have the ability to get your product out, license it, and develop strategic relationships for the revenue possibilities and for the credibility that brings. Often you'll want to give away limited rights to the company's technology that doesn't preclude the company from exploiting the intellectual property broadly and in a variety of areas. Not all can be foreseen on day one, so you often find yourself in situations where major players to whom you go for capital and strategic relationships and to obtain licensing royalties have been at this a long time. They know you're cash hungry, they know there's a great value to your being associated with them, and often they will reach for rights that are very, very broad. As you move forward, you find that some of your revenue streams are hampered by the fact that you've given away very substantial rights, including rights of first refusal. Thus for some modest initial gains, you've hocked your future. We've had a situation recently where a major technology company was going to make a $10 million investment and license a product that was not thought to be a dominant product for the client company. The $10 million wasn't desperately needed, the company had raised about $25 million in the prior year. The technology company, instead of just taking a limited license wanted broad technology rights that would have spread over into the products area more critical to the client company and rights that gave them exclusivity and long term lead positions. That would have dramatically hampered the client company's ability to score a home run. The deal ultimately floundered because it would have meant giving away a major portion of the value of the company for what was essentially a fairly modest equity contribution and insufficient minimum guarantees on royalties. That is something that one needs to guard against. At the same time, one needs to develop those strategic relationships. So it sounds like I've described a series of insoluble dilemmas. But that's inherent in trying to get money and trying to develop relationships on terms that are not unfair.

Biggest Mistakes New Companies Make

You can talk about a major mistake when somebody gives away too much intellectual property, or gives too big a piece of the company for the services or money it's getting, or gives an investor too much control which inhibits its future ability to raise needed funds in the second, third, or fourth round. Those are the major mistakes, in hindsight. Yet they're inherent in the situation, so to call them mistakes may be a misnomer. Some of the major problems that arise are giving away too much technology, too large an interest in the company, or too much control over future management decisions. Those are the major problems that arise in transactions that occur in the early life of companies, but they're not necessarily mistakes, they may have been compelled by circumstances. I have a view that the margin between floundering for lack of financial resources or strategic relationships and achieving the financing or strategic relationships that you need to have a very good chance to prosper and thrive is often very, very slim.

I represented one company that had a very good business model. They had already raised a few million dollars of early round angel financing. As they became more confident they added more staff, more technology capability, more programming capability, and they started running through their money more quickly than they had anticipated. They then needed to raise another $10 million to $15 million and the time frame that it takes to raise the money is invariably longer than the entrepreneur expects. It always takes longer. Maybe two of the biggest mistakes are not adequately anticipating how fast you're going to run out of money, and how long it's going to take to raise the next round of money. So they negotiated with five or six major financial institutions that were going to make investments and also joint venture to use the financial services products being generated by this new company. There came a point when the company had four weeks of life left. At the end of four weeks they would have been destroyed, out of money, and they would have been either totally unable to negotiate because they had no money or they would have been out of business. One or two of the prospective investors faded away, someone else took their place, and we ended up getting a major commitment from a very well known Wall Street investment bank. However, the investment was conditioned on having an aggregate investment in that round at a specified amount. The first investor did the deal on very fair terms; the second prospective investor came in for much less than the first investor, but somehow understood, without anyone telling him, that we needed his money even though it was less than the first investor's. Because this became clear to him, he ended up negotiating much harsher terms than the first investor. The company was probably within seven days of not being in a position to continue its business and having to lay off critical staff, as a result of which the company either would have gone bust or had to give away its business for next to nothing. The company was forced to accept very harsh terms. From there the company went on to enter some strategic relationships with these enterprises and moved to add additional investors in that round, without any additional pressure. That was a good illustration of the dynamics of needing the money, being put under time pressure, and having to give away a lot to get the money. I wouldn't say it was a mistake, but as time goes on there will be some constraints that will inhibit the company because of the terms it was forced to accept. Sometimes a company must make compromises because it has a desperate need for the money.

New Precedents Established From a Fund Raising Perspective

Some of the investors have been very aggressive in collateralizing some of the intellectual property in ways that ties the hands of the issuers, so the balance of power has changed. The second new thing we've seen recently is where the investor comes in, and in addition to getting standard anti-dilution provisions, they demand some price guarantees that provide that in the event of liquidation or some major capital event they will be entitled to a certain minimum amount of a priority return. This can be through warrants that guarantee the return or just an outright guarantee of that return. The effect is to create some extraordinary amounts of dilution for other investors in certain circumstances, because if things go poorly then the percentage of the company that can be owned by those new investors will be exceptionally high. That's something one would not give unless the company is hard pressed. Again, whether you call them mistakes or not, having more money than you think you need and perhaps giving up a little extra equity at the earlier stages to avoid being in a distressed situation at a later point is probably a good thing to do.

Partnerships

If a company enters a joint venture with another company with respect to some intellectual property that it owns and is collaborating with the joint venture partner to develop some special applications for use by them, the question who owns and who has the right to use the further intellectual property that is created through the joint activities is a very complicated area. Very often as you move forward with the partner in developing some specific application you create some valuable technology, and it's very important to retain the right to continue to use that new technology because where the ultimate pot of gold will be is often indeterminate at the early stage. If you look at business plans formulated in the first stage of a company's life, and compare it to the ultimate products and revenue sources, there often turns out to be a wide variance, not because of anybody's lack of vision or stupidity but because it's impossible to have sufficient vision to see where it's all going to end up. So you've got to be very careful about giving up intellectual property rights that you're not sure that you need on day one, because when you get to day 300 and 600 it turns out those rights are very valuable to your business. I think that's the hardest thing. In fact, a recent deal I described blew up over that issue. Again, it's a question of holding out. But if you're desperate for the money or you don't have any strategic partners, you're often in a position where you end up folding on these issues, and later, if things go well, you feel foolish for having given up too much. But at the time of the deal there may have been no choice.

Biggest Tax Consequences

I really haven't seen many issues of great magnitude in the tax area. One important issue that comes up is what type of entity to use. Should you use a corporation or a limited liability company ("LLC"). When you have a company that may have several business possibilities and you start a company in a corporate entity, when you later have the opportunity to spin off one segment of the business, if you're in a corporate structure the tax cost of spinning out the division is very significant.

On the other hand, if you use a limited liability company to start with, the ability to spin off one or several divisions is more favorable tax-wise and can avoid a huge tax at various corporate levels. There was a time when people though there were tax advantages to setting up as an LLC. After doing that for a while, we found ourselves in situations where the VC investors often came in later and felt it was too complicated and they wanted a simple corporation. So then we gravitated back to using the corporate form for simplicity's sake and anticipating the preferences of the VCs. But recently I've seen a number of situations where companies using a corporate structure have several divisions, and if they had been in an LLC form they would have been able to spin off the businesses in a way that is very tax effective.

There's also a major tax consideration involved in granting tax options below market value. Companies are under a lot of pressure to issue below market stock options to executives and to employees and the consequence of that is to have some ordinary income tax consequence rather than tax-favored capital gains treatment for the holders. Also, this can trigger a tax at the time of exercise of the option rather than at the time of sale. Again, it's not a question of mistakes. It involves balancing the desire for a cheaper option price against the resulting adverse tax consequences.

Another thing that happens in this context sometimes is that there are some significant expense recognition items for accounting purposes that are generated by stock option plans. If the stock option plan has a below market price or has a feature that allows the option holder to use appreciation of the stock option to pay for shares of stock, you are often required to revalue the stock option periodically and treat the enhancement in value as compensation to the employees and others receiving those stock options. The result is the company being required to recognize an expense item can run into the multi-millions of dollars when the company reports its earnings.

Biggest Misconceptions Regarding Stock Options

There is a lack of sophistication about the tax consequences. People have to think through carefully and understand the tax consequences. Most executives aren't aware of the accounting implications and the charge to earnings that will flow from many of the stock options they're granted. Sometimes in the early stages a young company wants to do things very cheaply and they don't want to spend a lot of time with lawyers or they're hiring lawyers who will work very cheaply and it won't be very sophisticated work. They will then end up doing some things that will have later consequences in terms of tax consequences to various parties and accelerated charges against earnings.

One other thing is very important. You have to be very sensitive on how you word the preemptive right protection granted to early stage investors. Preemptive rights entail a grant to a shareholder of rights to purchase additional shares in the event of future sales. If these provisions are not drafted carefully, it can be burdensome later on. I've seen situations where it's drafted poorly and the early money gets a chance to refrain from investing in the second, third, and fourth rounds and when the fifth round comes up they have the opportunity to recapture the same original percentage of the company owned by them, even though they haven't participated in rounds two, three, or four. If one is not careful that can give rise to some significant problems.

One must also be very careful in the early stages of raising money to think through all of the securities laws implications. If you do some careless private placements where you are not careful about the securities laws compliance in the early rounds of financing, then when you have a major opportunity to either raise money or to do a merger, you may find your new investor or merger partner unhappy because they see themselves as being subject to significant liabilities under the securities laws. There are private placements rules, called Reg D, which allow you to sell to a large number of accredited investors, i.e., people who have a million dollar net worth or income of $200,000 for several years. If all your investors are accredited, then you don't have to give them any special form of disclosure, even financial information disclosure, although you must avoid being misleading in what you do give them. But once you bring in some investors who are not accredited, and often that's the case with friends and family, you're in a situation where unless you give them very detailed disclosure, which is equivalent to disclosure contained in a public offering and in certain cases make sure they're represented by a "purchaser representative," then those offers are subject to other exposures under the securities laws. Later if you are doing a transaction involving a merger into another company, for which the acquiring company is issuing the stock in exchange for your shares, the buyer may be afraid to do the deal because of potential securities law exposure. I was in a situation where the company was being sold to a very promising technology company which was about to go public. The buyer, which was going public, was very sensitive about having any issues in their registration statement arising from the failure of the acquired company to comply with the securities laws, and was also concerned about the fact that the acquirer would be issuing its shares to people who were not "accredited investors." We ultimately solved the problem, but it almost killed the deal. The main lesson here is to be careful in every aspect of your fund raising. Even if the amounts are small, comply with the federal and state securities laws and go to the trouble of doing it right. It is a pain in the neck and it is costly when you have non-accredited investors. It may be best to avoid being a nice guy and don't allow your cousin and your friend in the deal if they're not accredited investors, because later on you may come to regret it.

Cost Effective Ways for Startups to Get the Legal Help They Need

First of all, it's not necessary to apply for 400 trademarks. I am amazed at how often I see these small Internet companies requesting us to work on numerous trademark applications in a multitude of countries. I find myself wondering why are they spending this huge amount of money. The company hasn't got two cents yet, they've got nothing to protect. While you want to be forward thinking and you want to protect some key names, there has to be some balance. On the other hand, you can argue that if the company turns out to be very successful and very prosperous and did not adequately protect the trade names, they may complain if the trademark protection is not exhaustive. The other dilemma I've seen repeatedly is this: on the one hand I've said you've got to be very careful, comply with the securities laws and be careful about the tax implications of your options plans. On the other hand, I've seen some companies that get excessively concerned with legalities. There's one new startup company we worked for and provided some standard formation documents. The founder said, "I don't want to do it the standard way." He got very complicated and very creative in the beginning which resulted in spending too much money on matters that were just inappropriate, given his financial capacity at the time. He should have done it straight forward in the first round and then added some fine tuning as time went on.

Protecting Domain Names

Everybody wants to protect their domain name, there's no question about it. One of the first things you must do is protect your domain name, and you must file some trademark protection. I'm just discouraging people who are going out to protect a multiplicity of trademarks before they've even done anything else.

The other thing companies need to do early on is develop a business plan. You don't need a business plan only to raise money. The business plan also helps you think through exactly what you're doing, what your revenue streams are going to be, what your priorities are, and how much money you need to carry out each aspect of your plan to earn revenues. If you can only raise $10 million or $20 million and your plan requires an expenditure of $50 million then you've got to make sure you're focusing your business on those aspects that can be pursued with the limited amount of money you're capable of raising at any given time. I think preparation of a business plan is an invaluable exercise and a lot of companies just aren't disciplined about it. They think it's just a piece of paper that you show to somebody to raise money. That's a total misconception. It's a fundamental part of figuring out your business in a way that will enable you to manage it sensibly.

Important Legal Topics Being Addressed

We're actually involved in Napster and in a major DVD encryption piracy case. We've been fortunate to be in several other cutting-edge cases. These cases have enormous legal and economic significance.

I think Napster's a huge issue. The extent to which traditional copyright laws are going to be respected and people who create intellectual property are going to have the value of their endeavors protected against is one of the major social, political, and legal issue of our time. There are major policy issues involved, and while there's tremendous demand that people simply be given free access, one could also argue that it's almost like stealing. If the various media and intellectual property rights belong to somebody, you can't take these rights without paying somebody for what belongs to them. The copyright laws have been developed to create incentives for certain kinds of original works and to foster the efforts in music, film and literature, and a variety of other areas, and it's a system that has worked. At the same time there's this massive demand to have access without paying for it. Video encryption and piracy of video product is another example. Once someone makes a movie, should the public have access to it and the right to make copies without paying somebody for it? If someone can just transfer music and videos what happens to the economics that generate all of this creative product? What happens to the incentives for people to create? Will it ultimately reduce the proliferation of these types of creative efforts that we're trying to encourage? It's a very interesting problem and it can't be solved in a minute and a half. We have recently seen some important negotiated deals in the music field that foster broad access on terms that compensate those who own the intellectual property in question.

Arnold Levine is a member of the firm's Executive Committee and recently served as co-chair of Proskauer Rose LLP's Corporate Department. He currently heads the firm's iPractice Group, which focuses on startup and development stage companies in online, Internet-based businesses and related technologies. Arnold has also been in charge of the firm's extensive activities in the field of partnership law, joint ventures, limited liability companies, private placements and syndications. In this connection, he heads up the corporate side of an interdepartmental team that has successfully completed over 500 syndications in transactions which have raised over $3 billion from investors and involved the acquisition of more than $20 billion of assets.

Arnold graduated from Cornell University and received his LLB from Columbia Law School, where he was editor of the Columbia Law Review. He has served as a trustee of the UJA - Federation of New York and as a director of the Mid-Westchester YM-YWHA, the Karen Horney Institute and the Henry Kaufman Foundation.

GORDON CAPLAN

Protecting Your Assets

Mintz Levin Cohn Ferris Glovsky and Popeo PC

Area of Expertise

I'm a corporate finance and technology lawyer, in addition to working with telecommunications companies. I focus on emerging growth companies and venture capital and private equity investments.

Interactions With Telecommunications Companies Versus Technology Companies

Telecommunications companies, especially some of the older, imbedded telecom companies tend to be much larger than the "new economy" technology companies. Although a lot of those telecommunications companies are rolling out new technology, they are doing it within an older utility-type environment. The new technology companies tend to be somewhat younger and more flexible but also a lot less experienced. Therefore, we have to provide a lot more advice and caring for some of the emerging technology companies while we don't have to provide that much hand-holding to the larger telecoms.

Biggest Issues Facing Technology Companies

Right now, the biggest single issue is lack of access to the financial markets: both the private equity markets and the public markets. Essentially the public markets have shut down a lot of Internet sectors and technology sectors, but the private markets are treading a lot more carefully than they had in the last two to three years. The single largest impediment to growth for good technology companies is a limited access to capital.

Biggest Issues Facing Telecom Companies

Actually, telecom companies are facing that same issue. Telecoms are getting a special pounding in the market place probably because money was freewheeling for large telecommunications build-outs in the last three to four years. There can only be so many competitors for the same business in the market place before it becomes a commodity and people start losing tremendous amounts of money.

The Legal Future

In particular, I think that the Justice and the FCC are not going to see the telecommunications companies as the big monopolies that they once were and that they do not have to fear their recombining. Also, open access rules are going to become even more important with respect to new technologies and gaining access to the individual in the home. The ultimate issue is the pipe into the subscriber's home or business. I think that the FCC is going to look more favorably upon aggregation while the market insists on open access.

The FCC had been afraid of consolidation to a certain extent, especially in telecommunications, because they looked at these companies with the traditional view that control of the long distance market really meant control of a significant piece of the telecommunications market. However, controlling the long distance market may be a negative for a telecommunications company and is not necessarily something that somebody wants a monopoly over. So I think that they are a few years behind in realizing that there are tremendous amounts of competitive pressure on the large telecommunications companies and that without some aggregation in the marketplace there's going to be a lot more failures than we're already seeing.

New Precedents

I think in particular the anti-trust decision against the World Com/Sprint merger is going to turn out to be not necessarily the best decision that has been made. I think there's going to be some realization that just allowing competition doesn't mean there will be competition. These markets are really cost prohibitive so you really need to have multiple lines of business to weather storms. Just because you allow competitive local exchange carriers to exist doesn't necessarily mean that they'll be good competition in any given market.

The Technology Company Difference

The problem is the belief that technology companies are different than other companies. I think the bottom line is you need good management and good blocking and tackling, which does not change whether you're in the car industry, the grocery industry or the technology industry. Obviously, intellectual capital is extremely important and has to be fostered in a flexible open environment. If that is in fact the case you still need good executing management where you have people on the management side and on the corporate finance side who know how to get things done. I would take a mediocre business plan with great management and great executors over a fantastic business plan and great technology with inadequate managers any day.

The Most Exciting Areas of Technology Law

I think health care and privacy issues are extraordinarily exciting. The emerging area of multiple access to subscribers and telecommunications is also very exciting. The FCC's decision on mandating carrier access to major real estate holdings is going to raise a number of constitutional as well as local issues with respect to property law issues and the constitutional issues. I think that the on-going debate about software patents and process patents is finally going to come to a head in the next year or so and we're going to see a more intelligent, more reasoned approach to issuing patents in those areas. I think those three or four areas are really where a lot of the activity is going to be in the next two to three years.

Major Issues in Mergers and Acquisitions

I think there's going to be a lot of issues relating to fiduciary duties of directors in connection with the sale of what are essentially insolvent entities. We are probably going to see a lot of that over the next 18 months as many high tech, formerly highflying companies essentially go bankrupt and/or merge and where the creditors' interests are not necessarily protected or the creditors' interests converge with the equity holders' interests. We haven't seen that in a while and I think that's going to be a really interesting topic for high technology M & A in the next 24 months. Another very interesting area is that M & A is going to be driven more by technology than it is necessarily by balance sheets. In other words, a telecommunications company may take over other telecommunications companies because they have compatible technology, which raises all sorts of intellectual property issues. This was the case in the Deutsche Telecom/Voicestream merger.

Advice for Internet Startups

Make sure that you know where your next or first "meal" is going to be coming from. Make sure that you can buckle down and focus not just on your next fund-raising opportunity, but getting cash flow and ultimately to positive cash flow. Keep your sites on a fairly focused area and understand that you may be in for a rough ride.

Biggest Mistakes Being Made

Certain dot.com startups have made one major mistake. The mistake has been believing that if you throw money at buying market share and at brand recognition, you ultimately will win. That is not how you build businesses.

For some reason people got away from the notion that you build businesses based on good management and good sales that are profitable. The goal should be positive cash flow not just market share. A company should grow because it's ultimately going to grow into profitable markets, not just because it's going to grow into a "first mover" advantage. I think the whole notion of first mover advantage is wrong and that often times the real successes are the third and fourth movers, who pick up the pieces afterwards.

Biggest Mistakes Established Companies are Making

I think essentially the notion that you could add dot.com to your name and become a high flyer. It's a mistake to ignore the Internet and to ignore what I think is a true shift, a revolutionary shift, in the way business is done. That's a mistake that a lot of companies have made. Another mistake is rushing into it with your eyes closed and just throwing money at any Internet and technology strategy. I think the ones like GE for example, that have been more reserved and waited for the dust to settle a little bit have been smart. GE has implemented its program from the bottom up, not from the top down, and they seemed to have focused on the technology, and have understood the technology that it is implementing. Really established companies with good management can execute on that technological strategy far more successfully than companies who just jump in because they think everybody else is.

Established Companies That Have Made Mistakes

There's a whole host of more established companies that have made mistakes. You could take a look at maybe half of the major media companies in this country, such as Disney and say that they made major mistakes on the Internet: thinking that they could just apply their existing media approach to an Internet approach which has a lot of fairly traditional content and a dial-up audience without focusing on the technology that is going to reach those people first and figuring out what content is best suited for that technology. I think there have been a number of companies that have made that mistake. On the other hand certain companies like AOL which is now an obviously more established company, have been very good about making sure that the technology is there before building the content around the technology that's applicable.

Important Things to Have in a Copyright Contract

I think what people often forget is that they have to know what the revenue stream is and the way to account for that revenue stream. It is very important to be able to have rights of insight, whether those are audit rights or other rights, to be able to look at what revenue is really being generated off of your intellectual property. Also, the ability to restrict the use of that intellectual property is essential because the more widely used it is, the more of a possibility that it's depreciated over time which should not be the case with well-protected intellectual property.

Protecting Software

If it is your software, you want to make sure that the software license agreements are well drafted and clear, the rights of use are limited, and that rights to modify are only given out in limited circumstances. You must have people that monitor those contracts and monitor your licensee's use of the software. At the same time, both for business operational and legal reasons, you want to make sure that you have the technical folks who are on top of the development of that software with the clients and/or licensees who are using it. This also allows you to keep in touch with what they are doing with the software. It is not only a matter of documenting correctly but also of keeping an eye on your asset.

Business Development Contracts

It depends if you're talking about a joint venture or a joint marketing arrangement. In the joint venture context it depends on what you are joint-venturing on. It's very important to make sure that you're not being treated like a new company, either for tax accounting or securities law purposes. It is also important to retain strict limitations on participant liability, and to ensure proper delineation and accounting of profits and losses. Again, a lot of joint venture agreements that we inherit after they've already been consummated are less than clear on those issues and that's where you see a lot of litigation, especially between startups, about who owns what and who's going to get what percent. Those kinds of things need to be clearly defined in advance by the business people, not just on the basis of a hand shake and simple agreement. On marketing, it's the ownership that is probably the most important thing, what are you marketing, who's going to own the brands that are marketed, and who's going to own that intellectual capital. I see a lot of litigation and dispute emanating out of these joint programs where it's not clearly defined who owns what and who's going to get what out of that program.

Employee Contracts

If you're the employer I think the most important thing to have is the ability to terminate without cause and without a significant penalty. Employers often think employment agreements are good for them, but that's not necessarily the case. We often advise clients that if you could stay away from employment agreements and instead have non-disclosure and non-compete agreements that it would be better. The other important issue, especially from an intellectual property perspective, is to have a good work-for-hire provision that clearly states who owns the stuff going on in people's heads and being developed while they're at work or within the scope of their employment for the employers. That's something that is often missed and there's a lot of focus on non-competition but not enough focus on work-for-hire arrangements. With respect to the employee I think employees often don't get good counsel because they don't want to spend the money. They don't want to spend time on defining what they do get and what they don't get in the form of equity and/or more traditional cash compensation in the event that they're terminated for any reason. It could be a termination because of a disability or death or more likely just a termination by resignation or firing. Employees don't focus enough on defining the "cause and not for cause" and I think that's an important thing for employees to make sure they're getting good advice on. Also, making sure that they don't get involved in broad non-competes is very important. Even if those non-competes are not enforceable or not clearly enforceable in any given state, new subsequent employers may want to avoid inheriting a lawsuit.

Investment Contracts

If you are the investor, you want to make sure that you have certain protections with respect to your investment. You want protections in the event they issue securities at a price lower than yours. You need the ability to stop certain issuer transactions if you think they are not in the best interests of the company or in the best interests of the shareholders. This is particularly important in private companies. Often times, a lot of thought and negotiation goes into things that are not nearly as important, like registration rights. On the issuer side, companies, especially in this market, are sometimes so desperate for money they don't realize what they are giving up. Even if they are not necessarily giving up 51% of their stock they may very well be giving up control of their company by way of negative protective provisions or negative covenants. These essentially give the investor negative control of the company. This can show up in all sorts of places in the investment documents. These provisions can show up in the registration rights, lock up agreements, and in the co-sale and drag along provisions. It is important for companies that are raising money to understand what that all means. It is also important to understand that preferred stock often has a dividend, and that dividends may be paid in more stock that can further dilute the founding or early shareholders. I think the investor class also has to be careful that its rights are preserved with respect to other investors. If you are the last investor to put in $10 million dollars into a private enterprise, you want to make sure that your rights are protected.

The Termination Clause

There should be clear termination rights for both parties, with respect to a joint venture arrangement and certain investment arrangements. Termination is often the best way to end the dispute. Business people, often do not like to think about termination provisions because they feel it is a down-side or "lawyers" issue. Well-constructed termination provisions may, however, allow people to walk away graciously without necessarily having a dispute.

Issuing Too Many Shares of Stock

Assuming that a company is private, they can run into significant Federal and state securities law issues if they start issuing stock to too many people. Dilution to early investors and shareholders should also be carefully monitored. Many public companies have lately been issuing a lot of stock into the public markets. However, the public markets at times failed to respond generously to those issuances and companies are trading at market capitalizations that are much lower than they were just months previously. The other aspect is that using stock as a currency to acquire companies is great but at the same time you need to make sure that you are not using all of your capital or significant portions of your capital to acquire things that are not core to your business. AT&T is a good example of this when it spent half of its capitalization to buy into the cable market.

Legal Agreements All Companies Should Have

Fundamentally, both public and private companies should have good underlying capitalization documentation. This means a good charter and laws that are in compliance with the local laws. Good minutes should be recorded because often, especially in fast paced private and startup companies, this is not done and has to be cleaned up at an extraordinary expense when the company wants to do something major like going public. I think it is very important for companies to have good non-disclosure, confidentiality agreements, and work for hire agreements with its employees. This is especially important with high technology companies because it enables them to hold onto the intellectual capital that the company is developing. It is also important for companies to take seriously their contracts with third parties, including vendors. Those arrangements can mean the make or break of small and mid-sized companies. If these contracts are badly structured a company could be in major trouble; whether it means not being able to get access to supplies when they need them, or being held up for money when they otherwise should not have to pay. I think some of these things are not necessarily paid as much attention to as they should be especially when they are most important, at the early and structural stages of a company.

Legal Issues That Can Haunt an Internet Company

There's a whole host of legal issues that can, and have come back to haunt a lot of Internet companies. These issues vary from infringement of other people's intellectual property, to the improper issuance of stock. Issuing stock to the wrong parties, and/or to too many parties and in the wrong way, or issuing stock to non-accredited investors at the early startup stage can really get a company into hot water. The infringement not only of other people's intellectual property but also of their business practices has wound up in court quite a few times. Recent examples include the lawsuits that emanated out of the Kosmo.com and Urban Fetch business plans in New York. I think that the more flexible and less formal work environments, although fantastic and often good for generating imaginative personnel, have to be watched with respect to things like sexual harassment and discrimination. This is still a professional environment and people need to act professionally.

The Importance of Confidentiality Agreements

It is important but often difficult to get potential investors, such as venture capital firms, to sign confidentiality agreements. I represent a lot of venture capitalists and institutions and I typically counsel that they do not sign confidentiality agreements because it is an invitation to a lawsuit. The real way for a company to protect their intellectual property, when they are raising money and bringing in new equity, is not by having everybody and their brother sign the investor confidentiality agreement, but by only disclosing what is necessary to disclose in order to entice them. You do not have to, nor should you, tell them everything about your underlying technology. Frankly, you may be wasting their time if you do. What you really need to do is get them enticed by the idea, enticed by the management and then they will have the right people come in and do the real technical due diligence.

Secondly, you should deal with people you know that are reputable and come from reputable sources or references. Companies should go to reputable venture capital firms, whether it's Kleiner, Perkins, U.S. Trust or Chase Capital

Partners because you can have some confidence that their main line of business is to help businesses grow and it is not to steal ideas. If venture capitalists get a reputation for theft like that, they will not be in business very long. Therefore, you can rely on reputation to a certain extent, and where you got the reference. Parties to commercial arrangements, such as vendor contracts, typically do execute mutual confidentiality agreements and this is appropriate.

The Importance of Trademarks

Trademarks are important. Attaining a trademark is fairly easy to do if you have something that is truly unique. The question is, however, what is the right business practice. It is extraordinarily expensive for businesses to succeed in creating brands. There are very few, really good knowable and instantaneously recognizable brands in the United States, despite what people think, and those brands, whether it's "Coca Cola" or "Tide," took years and hundreds of millions of dollars to develop. For dot.coms to believe that they could develop similar brands, with a lot of marketing and 30-second spots during the Super Bowl, was frankly pure hubris. This was encouraged by some of the financiers of these dot.coms.

Privacy Issues

I think privacy issues have had a huge impact already, whether you're DoubleClick, Amazon.com, or other Internet companies. I think these companies are not only being far more protective and far more serious about those issues, but there is going to be a lot more government regulation and judicial action in that area. These companies have to treat their customers and subscribers seriously, and I think most of the more well known companies are doing a great deal to try to make sure that their subscribers and their communities are protected, and the information about those individuals is not publicly disseminated without the subscriber's consent.

International Laws

People think that international laws are more complicated because they do not know them. In some areas, they are less complicated. European law, at least on domain names, is less complicated than it is here in the United States. I think that, with respect to development of wireless standards in Europe for instance, the EU has been more interventionists, but at the same time possibly more progressive than in the United States. There is going to be some convergence between the foreign and domestic laws especially among developed countries. It is going to be less a question of national versus international but that of developed versus non-developed countries. For example, in Russia it is far harder to enforce property rights whether it is a right in stock or a right in real estate than it is in Great Britain. That does not help the Russian economy, instead it hurts it significantly. Bankruptcy protection laws are different here than in Europe but at least they are fairly predictable. The real issue is not one of complexity. I think there is going to be more and more regulation, but it will, with respect to the developed world, continue to converge. Much of the undeveloped world, however, is struggling to enact and enforce those same types of structures so they will continue to be at a disadvantage.

The Legal Future for Internet Companies

I believe that there are going to be different tax laws with respect to e-commerce especially. I don't think that e-commerce is going to remain tax-free forever. Although my view on that is contrary to what other practitioners feel, I think that process and software patents are going to be looked at more carefully by the patent bar and the patent office is going to be less generous in these areas. Other intellectual property issues are going to be more clearly defined, for instance, in ownership and title. What's going to emanate out of the Napster litigation is really going to have a tremendous impact on traditional companies and new companies and there is going to be even stronger enforcement of copyright, trademark and other intellectual property protections, because that's really where people's capital is going to be based.

Gordon Caplan is a member of the firm's New York office, where he practices in the Business and Finance Section, focusing on technology and telecommunications related corporate matters, venture capital and mergers and acquisitions.

Gordon has extensive experience with corporate finance and general corporate representation of a number of public and private companies - including numerous high-profile companies - on a range of matters including private equity fundraising, contract, licensing, employment and other related matters. Gordon also represents a number of the leading private equity funds in and around New York that are investing in high-technology ventures.

Gordon serves as lead outside counsel to Sprint PCS in connection with some of its largest and most complex telecommunications infrastructure sourcing and licensing arrangements. He has also represented investors and issuers in over $1,000,000,000 worth of venture capital investments and offerings.

Gordon received his B.A. from Cornell University College of Arts and Sciences in 1988 and his J.D. from Fordham University Law School in 1991, where he was Editor of the Fordham Law Review from 1990-1991. He has published on the subject of high-technology transactions and has lectured at Columbia University Graduate School of Business on the subject of venture capital transactions.

JAMES HUTCHINSON

The Golden Rules of Raising Capital

Hogan & Hartson L.L.P

Background

Professionally, I started with Fried Frank, a big Wall Street firm in their Washington, D.C. office. It was '93 when I graduated from law school, so the economy had not fully rebounded. I worked on the insider trading enforcement action cases, Michael Miken/Ivan Boesky type cases, and the fallout of the roaring '80's. I did that for a year but figured out pretty quickly I didn't want to be a Securities litigator. I left Fried Frank and went into business with my college roommate. We started a small commercial finance company and built that up from the two of us to about 20 people in about a year. We went from a very small portfolio to one close to about $100 million. We sold out to a bigger finance company in Baltimore at the end of our first year in business. It was very condensed experience start to finish. We built real fast, we had really good marketing, and everybody knew about us in a short period of time, but we were definitely the small fish so we decided to sell.

After the sale of the business, I had a little bit of luxury to figure out what I wanted to do. I sought out a fairly unique legal position. I didn't want to go directly back to a big firm and be another grunt. I found these two guys, who were the D.C. office of a Colorado-based law firm. All they were doing was venture capital and private equity work for mostly Chicago based buy-out shops. This practice was unique to D.C. at the time, and it was great because I was the only associate. I basically got thrust into a position where I was doing everything. I quickly got enough understanding and experience to do a lot of substantive deal work while many of my peers were still working on closing checklists.

Our practice ultimately ended up at Hogan & Hartson. That was three years ago. Life is good!

Exciting Aspects of Working With Startup Companies

The technology client's people are typically high energy, they tend to be very demanding but still know how to have a lot of fun. Working with these types of entrepreneurs and managers becomes infectious and this makes the job seldom boring. Additionally, for the legal professional who works with so many clients, it's very rewarding to follow a company and do multiple deals with them and watch them grow. Growth stage companies tend to rely on their legal professionals for legal advice but often look for general business guidance. For the entrepreneurial part of me it is really very exciting to be an important part in the growth of a company and get a taste of the entrepreneurial spirit that drives these companies.

The Perspective From Having Started a Company

I think it was pretty substantial. You've got a lot of people who can tell you what the legal answer is, but when you're a small company the legal answer isn't necessarily the right answer. Regardless of what side you're on, you need to be able to be practical and understand how to best allocate resources. So I think it was actually really nice to have been part of a startup. It was tough at the time. Like any startup, I was everything from the general counsel to the office maintenance man. I think it gives you a totally different perspective, and also since my experience was fairly condensed, I got to see the full life cycle of a company. Business is tough. When you're a lawyer, particularly in a big law firm working for huge companies, you don't get a sense of how tough it is to be out there with everything on the line trying to make it happen. So I think it made me appreciate what entrepreneurs go through, the highs and lows, the risk. It made me a better lawyer because I looked for the pitfalls that weren't necessarily legal but more business focused. That's where I think the real value was.

Areas of Specialty

One focus is private equity, which in my mind means doing leveraged buyout work, rollups, leveraged buildups, and private mergers and acquisitions. Consolidation plays have been a big part of our practice the last couple of years. Wall Street has cooled to consolidations but there are a lot of mergers and acquisitions, a lot of management-led buyouts and heavily financed leverage deals still going on. Then the other half of what I do is pure venture capital work. Series A, B, and C financing rounds of companies that were either incubated by VCs, or a couple of smart people got together and convinced institutional money to come in. We represent money about 70 percent of the time, and then the small companies about 30 percent of the time. Many times we will become company counsel when our VC clients make an investment as well.

Typical Clients

One of the things you see is small companies that have a lot of money which allows greater use of expensive professionals. You didn't see that as much in the past. In addition, the level of technology companies we represent has increased dramatically. Tech companies are really driving much of the work we do. Finally, the amount of new VC money is staggering. Although venture capital financing has been around a long time, it's really bloomed in the Washington, DC area, particularly over the past five years. You had one or two outfits that did LBO work, but they weren't doing pure venture capital stuff. Now there are lots of VC funds of all different sizes and focus.

So you've got these small startup companies that instead of working in somebody's garage, they've got "Gucci" space and can afford lawyers and accountants because they've just been injected with $5 million in VC money. The good thing about it from a professional standpoint is that it allows you to do a better job for those folks because they can afford to do everything they need to do. The down side is it's amazing how much money gets wasted. By way of example, we have seen startup's that get $10 million in financing, (which is a nice day's work by anybody's measure) and they spend a million dollars outfitting office space. This in my mind seems like a bad allocation of resources.

Another downside to this situation is you see fairly inexperienced management teams with a lot of cash. VC's have so much money and there is real pressure to put it to work, I think it's a fairly significant difference than the entrepreneur who starts a business out of a garage, who didn't have any money and built a business with an eye towards profit. Venture funding came after the fact. Today you get a couple of smart people together who have a great idea, and up until recently have been able to persuade people to give them a lot of money, without it being completely clear that they can execute. They may be really smart and have a great idea, but the smartest guy doesn't always win.

Biggest Mistakes New Companies Make

I think the biggest mistake you see is people entering into agreements that have implications over the long term. When they've done a friends-and-family financing round that includes one or two clever investors in that round it can really create problems on the backside. For example, there's a story of huge telecom equipment provider located in our area, a Company with a multi billion dollar market cap. When it was just a handful of people and they were doing their startup financing, they signed a one-page letter with a small promoter who wanted to help them find money. They didn't let anybody look at the contract, and it had this tail that mandated that any financing that was done had to go through this guy. So every time they go to the public markets (equity or high-yield debt), he tries to hang up the offering. He gets paid to go away each time.

Startups are so organic, they change so quickly, that it's impossible to predict the future. When you get somebody asking to lock the Company up for anything for more than a year that sort of thing can come back and bite you. That's probably the biggest mistake that happens before they get to us.

The other thing is just being realistic. I have a client, a young guy. He is very smart, and he's got a great idea, but he's totally unrealistic about what it takes to execute a business plan and do all the things that have to be done to build a business. That's not so much a legal thing, but it has implications on what we do because he comes to us and he just doesn't have a realistic understanding of what it is that we can do for him, how long things take and how much it costs. We have seen a lot of startups choke when they get our first $40,000 bill from us. It was amazing how folks use lawyers differently after that first big bill or that first financing transaction falls apart.

Focal Points for Startups

The biggest thing is making sure you're very clear on who owns the company. People will issue stock here and there, give somebody a warrant, etc. The venture capitalists are buying a piece of the company. They want to know exactly who owns it and exactly who has rights to get equity, be it options, warrants, or convertible debt. In terms of the other housekeeping, board resolutions, contract management and keeping a tidy corporate house have important roles. When professional money comes in, the image that you project is very important. Lawyers and accountants go in and do due-diligence on a company the VC's are looking to invest in. When you get a box full of unorganized contracts, some signed and some not, everybody's antenna goes up. The process takes longer and it costs more if the legal house is not in order. I've been through this a number of times, and when you send the due-diligence request list and you get back organized binders, everyone immediately is a little more at ease because they think they've got everything together. But if somebody is not organized, the lawyers and the accountants can really start to breed doubt if they feel like the corporate house is a mess, particularly if it's not clear in who can get ownership rights and under what circumstances. Those are the type of issues that get the lawyers and than ultimately venture capitalists worried.

Equity Ownership

Equity incentive is extremely important. People have left promising old economy careers to take a flyer because they think they can get a lot of options. The equity component of the compensation has really become a key driver. Cash is no longer king if the options are there.

Have the laws changed? There are some things that have changed and that are changing on the tax front to deal with this change. The way vesting is treated and tax deferral under approved option plans is continuing to develop.

However, on the business front what is amazing to me is how little the average person understands about what they're getting. There are surveys that show the great majority of all options exercised result in ordinary income treatment to the holder, which is completely counter to the goal of incentive stock option plans and the relief provided under tax laws. If used right, incentive plans allow employees to get paid with equity, defer immediate taxes and then ultimately receive capital gains treatment. So you're talking about the difference between a 20 percent tax and almost a 40 percent tax. It can be a fairly substantial amount. It's just interesting when everybody's pulling for that golden option ring but they're not really cognizant of what it means.

Different Ways to Issue Stock Options

You know there's probably less than five different ways. It's remarkable how uniform it has become. In the mid-Atlantic region literally nine times out of ten you will see a four year vest, with 25 percent of the stock vesting at the end of the first year (a cliff vesting) and then monthly thereafter. Almost every deal is like that, which to me is sort of funny. If I'm in a tight labor market and I want to attract good people, and people care so much about the options, being aggressive with options would be an easy way to distinguish yourself. It's remarkable how infrequently it happens. However, Silicon Valley seems to lead developments on these issues. One of our biggest clients just went into business a couple of months ago.

They got $200 million of financing in April, and they filed to go public on the last day of September. They were billed as the largest first round VC financing ever at $200 million. Typically options vest over time. We represented the management team, and they have structured their incentive stock options for their core first-round employees so that they "reverse vest." Employees get immediately vested options that are then subject to repurchase by the Company. They were granted an option the day they started, it was immediately vested, and the company lent them money to exercise. The beauty of this approach is the holding period to ensure capital gains treatment start sooner than it would with a traditional option grant.

Other Important Issues

I think you do need a good business plan and you need to be smart about who reads it and how it gets read. If the top partners are not reading your business plan, there's a guy right out of MBA school or an ex-investment banker, a lower-level analyst or associate who's taking the first crack at reading your business plan. Knowing that, it's remarkable to me how many businesses I have seen that I don't understand exactly what they're doing and how they plan to make money. I think people need to be a little more careful about who the reader is and the fact that these places get thousands of business plans a week. Try to distinguish yourself a bit by having a really good executive summary. One of the things that we've been seeing a little bit more of, which I think is handy, is a corporate profile, a slick one pager, that sums up the company. You see entrepreneurs using more and more of that approach as opposed to a full-blown business plan, which you need to have but may not get read in its entirety. You need to do it short and sweet, so that's the first thing.

The second thing is not to underestimate relationships with professionals, both lawyers and accountants. Often we can open a lot of doors for people, we can get a company a meeting with somebody at Goldman Sachs, that they probably couldn't get on their own. It's important to leverage off those relationships.

Finally, be realistic. Raising capital doesn't happen overnight. And if you get yourself in a bind where you need money quick, that's death, because if you look desperate, you're not going to get money from anybody. So if your business model is such that you're out of money before you start looking for it, you're finished. The time to go look is when you're strong and you don't need it. It's silly but it's reality. People who don't need money have the easiest time raising it.

Smaller Versus Bigger Deals

A big deal is just not going to happen that fast, and it drives the entrepreneurs crazy. When the numbers are bigger, it really slows the train down substantially. A smaller deal (less than $5 million) done by a big sophisticated VC fund can be done, start to finish, in 3 to 4 weeks. With bigger numbers, people's reputations are at stake. So the big transactions just take more time and it's not necessarily any more complex, but everybody kicks the tires more.

The Ideal Lawyer

If I were sitting on the other side of the table, the first thing that I'd look for is just somebody I like, that you can have a conversation with, that you can go out and build a rapport with. To me that's the most important thing, because you can't woo anybody with the money that you've got necessarily because you're a startup. You need to leverage other things to get prime billing in terms of where you fall out on the importance scale. The startup needs to find somebody that's excited about business. If your professionals are committed to the idea on an emotional level, the service is likely going to be better. Its human nature. Find a professional that likes you and like your business. Additionally, I think its important to build the best team you can. If your professionals are from the top name firms you add creditability and legitimacy to your project.

Certain Areas That Need Specific Attention

IP, IP, and more IP. Intellectual Property is the heart of many tech companies so it is very important to protect it. You need good intellectual property counsel to get the VCs comfortable that your IP is protected in some fashion and that you alone can make money off of it. I think software companies in particular have the hardest issues. Open source companies for example are intriguing business models that provide real challenges in protecting IP.

What Bankers and Venture Capitalists Want

They do like to see something proprietary, something that everybody else doesn't have. Here's an example: we have a client now that has a software that's artificial intelligence, triggered off voice recognitions. It's really neat stuff. We introduced them to a couple of VCs, and one of the premier groups came back to us and said, "We've seen lots plans in the past six months and this is by far the most interesting." This is fairly logical and predictable because companies that have something that nobody else has get investors very excited. That's true even if there is not a great management team. The VC's can find strong managers to build a company around premiere technology.

Best Traits in Management Teams

I think depth, not just to have a strong finance guy or strong technology guy. The companies that are knocking the cover off the ball are coming pre-packaged to the money. Basically every facet of the business is wrapped up with really experienced people. Those companies are the ones that you really see succeeding in raising the money. Additionally, the serial entrepreneurs. If an entrepreneur has successfully built a company the playing field changes. The investment becomes less of a bet and the leverage changes.

I think the days of really young entrepreneurs getting a lot of money are gone because of the most recent market adjustment. The VCs have seen a lot of the waste and inability to execute. That is why you see the fairly regularly guy that started the company dropping out and the investors bringing in professional managers. In terms of having a proprietary product, that's one thing, but having a really seasoned management team is hard to do when you're a startup. How do you get seasoned people to sign on? That's the catch-22. But I think it's going to be particularly hard for young entrepreneurs to attract serious money without some gray hair professional managers as part of the team. We're seeing it more and more. And we're even seeing it when the VCs are making their first investment. The VCs are typically replacing the founder, putting him or her on the board, and filling out the management team with people they know.

Confidentiality Agreements

I think confidentiality agreements are important but they are, in my experience, rarely invoked. You need them, but at the end of the day what are you going to do with it? You can sue on it, but they're not typically non-compete and you can't keep somebody from going off and doing what you do or stopping a VC from making an investment in a competitor. They just can't use your information to go do what you do, and so they're fairly hard to enforce. So the real value is just the fact that there is a peg to hang your hat on in case you need to go back and contest, but that rarely happens. The reality is don't tell people things that you don't want them to know.

In terms of employment agreements on the other hand, I think those are extremely important. If you were to do a venture capital round of financing, you would hire lawyers to represent your company. However, it's important to remember, company counsel does not represent management. Company counsel gives some pointers to managers in their employment agreement, but at the end of the day the duty of the lawyers is with the company, not necessarily the managers. Sophisticated managers know this and get somebody to fight their fight just on the employment front. During a transaction, everybody gets so busy doing the deal, if there's not a person that's just focused on the employment agreement those issues can get moved to the back burner and the executive will lose leverage. As the company's counsel, it's hard to hang a deal up over employment agreement issues because you don't represent the employee. Other things like option agreements you really don't have that much leverage to negotiate. Sometimes you can win the day and get something a little different, but the VC's argument is, and it's a fairly persuasive one, "this company is going to have a lot of employees, we can't cut a million different deals."

Big Legal Issues on the Horizon

You hear a lot about privacy issues from the press, but from a practical standpoint you don't see much of it on the deal side. It's bantered around out there but usually the biggest action item is to require the target company to put its privacy policy on its Web site.

In terms of other global issues, intellectual property is always important as well as protecting trademarks, protecting trade names, and protecting software. Other than that, for the business terms of a financing there's a well-defined menu, and all the professionals know what it is, including the VCs. You pick one out of column A and one out of column B and go down the line like that. It is important to have experienced legal counsel not only to protect your interests but also to advise as to what is market.

Mr. Hutchinson is a senior associate with Hogan & Hartson, LLP in Washington, D.C. He received his B.A. from the University of Pennsylvania in 1988 and his J.D., cum laude, from the Georgetown University Law Center in 1993. His practice focuses on corporate transactions including venture capital financings, mergers and acquisitions, leveraged buyouts and other corporate finance transactions.

JOHN IGEO

Identifying the Right Legal Challenges

Encore Development

General Counsel

General Counsel Versus Working at a Firm

It is not really as large a change as I first thought it would be. I slowly had transitioned into this role. My last year at my previous job I was wearing lots of different hats while advising my clients. When I was a partner in the corporate finance department, we focused on clients in the public utilities and insurance industries. Around 1997 the firm started looking at emerging technology in high growth companies, especially in the regional offices. I found that they looked to me as their primary source of legal assistance. Most of my clients would look to me as their corporate counsel, as the primary conduit.

Most Important Issues as General Counsel for a Company

The first thing you have to do, as counsel, is to know your client. Then you must know the industry or business that the client's in, and try to get a handle on what the different risks are that the client faces as well as the different opportunities that they're confronting. This enables you to do several things. First, you can make sure the company has the proper insurance coverage. Often times in house legal counsel will be the sole risk manager, and they will be responsible for interacting with the outside insurance providers. Here we've got another person in that capacity. You must also make sure that your assets are protected. If you're in a business that is heavily dependant on intellectual property, you need to make sure that your patents, copyrights, or trademarks are strong and are protecting your property. In this business, one of our most valuable assets is our people resources, therefore we need to make sure that they are happy and that they are committed. We do this through incentives such as the stock option program. We also have employment contracts with key officers and employees, and we make sure that they've entered into the proper non-compete, work for hire or proprietary information agreement. This makes it clear that the work they're developing here is our work product so if they should ever decide to leave there's no question about who owns the information. This ensures that our assets don't walk out the door. Granted, it is hard to replace a consultant that is an asset that does walk out the door every night, but the intellectual property associated with what he, she and the others have collaborated on can protect you somewhat.

Most Important Issues to Farm Out to External Legal Help

Well, I think it comes down to two factors. The first is your expertise, and the second is your time. No one is an expert in all areas, and you need to have some self-awareness of what your own skills are and your comfort level with various topics. You must also be aware of your availability with regard to time. There's a lot to be said for managing costs and saving costs by doing things in house, but if you find that you can't address things in a timely fashion, your client, the internal constituent, is going to become dissatisfied and you will not serve them properly.

Biggest Issues Companies are Facing Today

The biggest issues I think that this company and others like us are facing are attracting and retaining employees and staying ahead of the technology curve. In the consulting business if you are not up on the latest technologies your company will soon find that they become a commodity if their margins go down, they will no longer be attractive to outside investors, and it will have a hard time retaining employees. Everybody wants to work for a successful company. People associate success with maintaining a high profit margin and working on cutting edge things. This is what helps to attract and retain employees. It's tough to always find employees that have those cutting edge skills but by focusing on those cutting edge areas it helps to attract those employees that do have those skills, because they know that they do have the opportunity to use those skills and learn additional skills as well.

Biggest Legal Issues

Online privacy probably touches on my company's business the most. This issue has been evolving through various regulatory and legislative efforts. There's been a lot of talk about regulation, but the standards haven't been set. We are all operating in a gray area. I think as a consulting firm this is a great challenge. Our clients direct us as to what they want to achieve, but we need to be cognizant of what the law is so we can help steer them.

Deciding When to Hire General Counsel

I think every company comes to that decision at a different point in time. What I believe will drive that decision-making process is cost, how much they are spending on outside counsel, and whether they can save any cost by bringing some of that function in house. I think a lot of company's in house accountants will approach that decision from that prospective, but I think most companies take a different approach in determining that it's a management issue. They feel that they have so many issues that need legal review, or legal counsel, that they need a lawyer in house that they can walk down the hall and talk to. I always pride myself on being available for my client, but there is a big difference between being available via the telephone, and being right down the hall. I think that there is a lot of value that an in house lawyer can bring to a company. They provide not only sound legal advice, but they also are able to apply that advice in the proper context. Oftentimes as outside counsel you are not kept up to speed on what the various business issues are so when you are presented with a legal question, you don't have the proper background or the proper understanding of the facts to give the best advice. I think there's a lot to be said for hiring in house counsel as companies consider going forward in their evolution and feel that they're going to be a publicly traded company one day. Especially counsel with some securities expertise and who will not only assist with that process but the post IPO process as well.

Identifying Troublesome Legal Matters

If you are a software manufacturer you want to make sure that you have the proper copyright protection of your software product. There is a business methodology associated with your product, therefore you want to make sure you have the proper patent. If you are a software-consulting firm, or a computer consulting firm like we are, you want to make sure that you have the proper non-competes with your employees, proper incentives, and work for hire agreements with your employees since they are your key assets. I've often seen a situation where a company has entered into a financing transaction with a VC firm or an angel investor where they have basically given away the ship, and they do not have the flexibility to bring in that next round of financing.

Partnership Agreements

The agreements need to be clear. People need to understand exactly what they're getting into. Myself and other lawyers often provide translation services. Business development people, or other executives at a company, will speak in a language they feel is clear, but it will be a language that can be interpreted a number of ways. When you actually put pen to paper and write an agreement you'll find the parties have differing views on what is really being said. Making sure everyone is clear is obviously paramount. The key provisions that I think are important are obviously termination provisions, and what type of notice provisions is associated with that. Often times, in this particular business, we need to commit resources to a particular project, and I think that clients and a third party have the right to terminate that quickly. We need to have some type of 60 or 90 day notice provision whereby we can transition our resources to other projects so that we can recover our investment. In addition, I think that there needs to be some clear understanding of who owns the work product. Do we have the right to use the product or certain parts of that product, and do we have a license to use that product afterwards? This is key.

With regard to the employee asset, both sides usually want some type of non-solicitation provision so that their assets aren't being raided by their partner. I think most prudent business people would not raid their partner of employees. Every now and then that does occur so I think parties should try to protect themselves in that area.

Challenges in a Financing Event

If you are outside and being brought in on a particular financing, it's a real challenge to be able to consummate the financing in a proper time frame and be cognizant of the prior agreements. Fortunately that is not an issue here because I have been fortunate to help the founders develop their equity positions and create a stock option plan. This plan ensures that proper incentives are given to employees, making sure undue dilution does not occur from the third party investor standpoint. I also help to bring in the venture capital financing to companies in their early stages. When you are involved in negotiations with outside investors they are going through an education process as well as far as determining how their investments should be structured. They are cognizant of prior investments so that is a helpful process to be involved in every step of the way.

Making sure that they enter into financing agreements that are flexible and permit future growth of the company as well as future financings is also an element that's often over looked.

The Interesting Part of New Legal Issues

Well for non-lawyers they are going to be surprised that any part of the legal profession is exciting. I think the biggest change is people's expectations. The past three years there has obviously been a change in the speed by which people expect to consummate transactions. For example, the speeds that they expect documents to be produced and the speed at which they expect to grow a company to reach liquidity are unprecedented. This is not so much a legal development, but a development that lawyers have to deal with. I think lawyers have to be cognizant of the change of expectations but they also have to be advising their clients to operate on a reasonable timetable. So many people read *Red Herring* or *The Wall Street Journal* and expect that once they come up with the idea to incorporate a company they should be doing an IPO in twelve to eighteen months. Clearly there are examples of that, but those are rare exceptions. I remind my clients that growing a company is difficult. I have to repeat that mantra often enough so that it sinks in without losing the client because clients expect their lawyers to perform, but you need to make sure they have the proper expectations. It requires time and nurturing to be able to make sure that my clients succeed. Companies need to keep their eye on the ball regarding the growth of their business. They need to pull the trigger at the proper time, but so many clients are being wooed to New York to attend IPO boot camps by various investment firms. They get caught up in that and forget that they need to have the infrastructure in place to manage their existing business and to allow growth. Then they can address the issues of what it is like to be a public company. That is an education process that lawyers have to provide their clients. Fortunately most clients are receptive to hearing this lesson and appreciate knowing what the process should be.

Doing Business Internationally

When you do business internationally, there are obviously additional laws and regulations that you need to be aware of. You also have cultural differences that you need to be aware of when negotiating transactions. The management must be prepared for increased travel as well. I think that it is one thing to worry about the logistics of having to fly East coast to West coast, etc., but to have to fly across the Atlantic or Pacific can be a hurdle. Here at Encore we have some international growth opportunities but we have not actually pulled the trigger on any of those yet. That is something that we will be facing fairly soon I think.

Advice for Internet Startups

Find a lawyer who has experience and expertise in your area. I think having someone with a corporate background is very helpful, but that person needs to have the ability to pull on resources that cover other HR and intellectual property issues. Corporate counsel often does not have sufficient understanding of securities law. If they don't I think that Internet startups should go elsewhere. I think an Internet startup should look at finding legal counsel like a marriage. They are going to be interacting with that person on a very frequent basis and they need to be comfortable with their legal skills as well as their personality. Some of the larger firms out there have wonderful resources, but if you cannot call upon them with the frequency you need that firm isn't appropriate for you. I think it is fair to have an initial discussion about the availability of counsel.

RICHARD TURNER

The Importance of Patents

Sughrue, Mion, Zinn, Macpeak & Seas

Senior Counsel

Background

I received a BS in Physics from Rensselaer Polytechnic, which is a technical university in upstate New York. Following that, I did a brief stint at Lincoln Labs over at MIT, but quickly decided that the lab coat was not for me. This was in the late '70's, and at that time many of my contemporaries were moving into research positions in the national labs to work on highly classified work in the nuclear area. I didn't really care for that either. I was looking for something else that fit with my technical background. I wandered into patent law, which is not that uncommon by the way. There are a lot of people that end up making that same kind of switch. I went to law school at George Washington University in DC. I was going to classes at night and working at the Patent Office during the day. In the beginning of my third year of law school I left the patent office and began working in my current law firm, where I found that my technical background lent itself to a variety of disciplines, including semiconductors, communications, software and optics. I still work in these areas today. Over the years, it seemed like each of these areas in turn experienced a "hot" period, though more recently all of them have exploded at the same time.

Changes in the Past Years

I've been pleasantly surprised, to be honest. Some of the companies that I see are very new, often they are not even officially formed yet. Despite that, there seems to be great appreciation among these companies for the value of patents. They realize that if you can't protect your core technologies and have some ability to keep competitors at arm's length, then you're not going to get very far. Some people have said, well we have an advantage because we were the first ones to get started on this and it's such a labor-intensive process to get to where we are, therefore we have the advantage. Of course that's a good business strategy, but if you don't watch your back side, and protect your advances as you progress, then other people will follow the same path and get there even if they're not first. And they might be better on the business side than you are. Amazon is one of the companies that has tried to protect the rungs on the ladder as they went up. Witness their successful suit against the other online bookseller, Barnes & Noble. I can cite them as a company that was smart enough to see that the business model by itself was not sufficient to secure the win in their space. They also had to protect things as they thought of them as they went along. I applaud that kind of effort.

When the Internet started to really move in about 1995, I had no intention of becoming an "Internet lawyer." I got pulled in that direction a little bit as I had clients who were getting to the point where they needed money. I was also at the point where I was doing some private investing. One thing led to another and I made connections with a lot of venture capitalists in this area and the angel groups and so forth. There was a kind of a serendipitous cross pollination for me where I learned enough about raising capital that I could help advise new startups on where to look, make introductions, and that sort of thing. I knew enough about technology to help the venture folks understand what they might be buying into as well. Networking is essential to this sort of deal making.

Important Issues - Patents

It's extremely important that companies file for a patent right away and for a number of reasons. The first is that the patent system generally rewards the person who comes forward first. The whole idea of the patent system is that you give up your idea to the public and in return you get a term of years during which you have exclusive rights over that property. Essentially, it's a contract with the government. If there are two players in the same space and they're coming up with the same advances at the same time, then generally speaking the first one to run to the patent office is going to be the owner of that technology. The second player is going to have to work it out with the first player. Obviously, from that perspective the first player has potentially a lot of power. Certainly, once they've obtained their patent and it is clear that nobody else has actually preceded them in the space, then they're going to be able to have monopoly power on that technology. Obviously that's a very powerful thing.

New Precedents

Companies are trying to protect themselves in a new way and to clear out space for themselves, in order to operate free of competition. Taking the Amazon case as an example, everybody says it's the patent on one click shopping, but there's technology behind that. It just wasn't simply the idea that they tried to patent, which is sometimes the case with the business model patents. I wouldn't classify Amazon's one click patent as a pure business model type of patent. It's clearly a business model based technology patent and as we in this business were pleased to find out. Amazon obviously believed that that process gave them a competitive advantage in the shopping space. I believe that it actually does just that.

New "Patentable" Areas

As with all new areas, it will take time to sort through the good from the bad. For example, the whole idea of business model patents is very new. There was a court decision fairly recently which opened the door for that type of patent, which was not necessarily technologically based.

There are business model patents out there that are not worth the paper that they're printed on. From my perspective, simply taking an idea that already existed in the business world and translating that to the Web is not patentable It's simply a transformation of an old idea into a new arena. In my mind, that should not be a patentable advance. The patent office in the early days, without very much guidance and without any ability to search out and discover business methods already existing, issued a bunch of patents that are very suspect in terms of whether they're actually valid or not. They've tried to correct that, but they're still behind the curve. With business model patents I think the adage is buyer beware. Even though you have your patent, whether it's worth something is somewhat debatable at this point. I'm talking about the pure business model patents in this discussion, the ones that are not technologically based.

New Precedents That Have Affected Patents

In the software area there's a substantial backlash among certain contingents of people who either believe that software should essentially be free or that patents are being used to kind of stifle their creativity. Some people would agree that either software should not be protected to the extent that it is, or if it is protected, it shouldn't be for such a long period of time because it's such a transient technology. In some respects that is true. However, I think that the Y2K problem proved that some types of software have longer lifetimes than anyone ever expected.

New Hot Spots in the Patent Area

I would have to say that various ASP models are very hot in the software area right now. Whether they're couched as a business model or whether they are actually technology solutions probably varies from company to company and from patent to patent, but there are a lot of companies that are hitting that space right now. The Internet opens up new possibilities for distributed computing, and there are a few companies starting to get moving there as well. In terms of hardware, the hot spots vary from year to year, but one of the areas that I think will see dramatic advances in the next several years is storage technology.

The Patent Process

Some of these things are kind of boring, but I first have to be sure that it's really their idea. Second, I have to be sure that it wasn't an idea that they developed while they were working for somebody else who may have some potential ownership rights. Once you past those two hurdles, then the question becomes do you try to do a search to see what other people have done in the same space or do you simply forge ahead? The cautious man says, do the search and see what else is out there. However, technology searches, particularly in the patent arena, are not necessarily 100% reliable. The reason for that is that the patent office holds applications in secret. Therefore, the snapshot of the public information that you get is 1 ½ - 3 years old. The window to the most recent developments is essentially opaque. Even if you do get a search that shows nothing there, you can't be sure that somebody else has not already applied for a patent on it. It is somewhat of a gamble, but it is a gamble that invariably pays off if you're right.

Eventually, this will change to a degree, since the patent office will start to publish most applications, beginning next year.

Making Money From Patents

People obtain patents because they want a monopoly position in a valuable technology. It may turn out that if the field is crowded, the monopoly you receive is very limited. Or, it may turn out that there are many alternatives to your technology, which diminishes its value. On the other hand, the pioneering patent in a widely adopted technology is a very valuable thing. You might think of Polaroid, who has cleared out a space that no one has been able to enter, instant photography. You can think of Texas Instruments as a different example. Jack Kilby just won a Nobel Prize. He was the first one to come up with the idea of the integrated circuit at Texas Instruments back in the 1970's. Now TI didn't try to monopolize that space themselves, but they did license the industry as it grew up. They obtained huge amounts, billions of dollars in royalties from other companies over the years who also wanted to be in the business of developing and selling integrated circuits. Had TI taken a different route and tried to keep all of that for themselves, I'm not sure they would have been able to do it. That area has become so big that if it were dominated by one company, then there would definitely be an anti-trust problem. So TI took the reasonable step and decided to license it out and get rich off of the industry's efforts.

Most Exciting Parts of Patent Law

The reason I got into this business was because I didn't want to lose the technological edge that I had from my formal training. I go home from my job every day having learned something and having seen the latest new thing I work close to the bleeding edge of technology advances, not just in one area, but in many. There is definitely a technological boom going on right now, and being close to the center of it is what makes me excited.

New Problems With New Clients

The Internet explosion has caused everybody to be in a hurry, so when new clients come to me with a new idea they're usually in a rush. They want to get something filed with the patent office right away and that's the smart thing to do. For patent attorneys, like me, it's difficult to maintain the bandwidth to handle all these urgent requests every day. The new technologies have forced patent attorneys to work at Internet speed to keep up with their clients. In the old days, if somebody brought you a new patent application, you said well, I can probably get this done in two or three months. That would have been completely satisfactory. If you were to tell that to one of my startup clients today, they would look at you like you were insane. Who would blame them with the situation that we have now? It has put the extra burden of speed on my profession, which wasn't necessarily there in the old days.

Pioneering New Space Within Patent Law

The major problem that I see is that companies will come to me with an idea, so focused on executing their technology, and to some extent their focus gives them blinders. They don't see the different uses that their invention may have other than the one they're working on. To some extent, one of my difficulties is in trying to fathom for myself the other applications an invention may have and bring it to their attention in hope of getting them to think about the broad horizon of applications that the invention might have and not just the one. Certainly, the Internet has caused us to think about business in an entirely different way. People are creating new businesses that would not have been possible even five years ago and that forces us patent attorneys to think outside the box sometimes. The burden is to try and fashion the protection for these companies. In some cases you try to forge new ground in the type of protection that you request.

Types of Things Clients are Trying to Patent

In general, I can tell you that the business model area is still very hot. These are going to be increasingly difficult to patent because they're being exposed to increasing levels of scrutiny within the patent office owing to some of the bad press that the patent office has gotten. On the whole, though, that's a good thing because there is nothing more harmful in this business than a rich company waving a bad patent. The cost of patent litigation is so high that anybody who has a patent has a very strong weapon that they can wield. There is a lot of competition out there and someone with a lot of backing and a bad patent can cause more damage to an industry than they can do good with it.

Litigation from start to finish costs at least $1 million dollars and can easily double or triple that. I've seen cases that were running almost $1 million per month. No matter who you are, those are obviously high stakes, and smaller companies don't have the wherewithal to fight those types of battles.

Small Companies and Patents

I should say by and large that the larger companies are very respectful of patents. If you're a little guy and a big guy is starting to get his toes into your turf and you've warned them and called attention to your patent, usually the result is that you will enter into some kind of discussion that will result in a solution. They will enter into some sort of intellectual exercise with you to find out what protection you're actually entitled to. There are a lot of good faith negotiations going on out there, even as we speak, and ultimately once the large company has settled on what the proper patent coverage might be, then they will either back off or they will license the technology. Having said that, there are some highly competitive companies out there, including one whose chairman is on record as saying, we're going to do what we're going to do and patents be damned. That sort of attitude is obviously a problem for everyone. Patents have a strange kind of momentum. If you have a patent and you're successful in licensing one partner and then one or two others, then you have momentum. Other companies coming into the space will see that well-known company A is licensed and well known company B is licensed. How much effort do you think they're going to go through to find out whether they should take a license or not? They're not. They will try to negotiate a good price. They will not necessarily try to mount a challenge. I know some companies that automatically build in a 7-10% royalty figure in their pricing model for every new product. This is before anybody has challenged their product. It's just that the contingent royalty cost is already built in. If it's never needed then it adds to the bottom line. If it is needed, then they've already taken it into account. It's probably a smart thing to do, but it sounds sort of defeatist.

International Patent Law

Well, essentially every country has it's own domestic patent law and none of them are precisely the same. Their standards may be different. The way they enforce them may be different. The way the rights accrue and the bundle of rights that you get might be different. There has been a move in the patent area for a generation to harmonize the laws of the various countries. Largely that movement has been successful, which is not to say that every country's law is now the same because they're not. There is somewhat more uniformity in the standards for granting patents and somewhat more uniformity in what you can expect out of an enforcement action. Those are really the two most critical areas. Things like procedure and so forth do not matter so much.

Challenges in Enforcing a Patent Internationally

Let me explain that the first step for U.S. companies is usually acquiring their U.S. patent, or at least applying for it. Now, by international treaty you're entitled to file your application in many other countries throughout the world within one year of that time without any consequence. What I mean by that is, other countries will treat it as if you filed it on the day you filed your U.S. application. That's an international treaty that over 100 countries have signed.

So close to a year after you've filed your U.S. application you have to make a strategic decision on what other countries you'd like to file in. Basically, you're going to try to predict where your market is going to be and go there. Let's say that you've acquired your patent in the U.S. and some years down the road you acquire your patent in Japan and now Sony is infringing your patent. You need to go after them. The situation is quite different in that country as opposed to here. Unlike the U.S., Japan is not a litigation-oriented society. In fact, it's quite the opposite. It's more of a mediation and consensus based society. Until recently, filing suit in Japan was viewed as an admission of failure, meaning that the social network or the social bias toward mediation, accommodation, and resolution of disputes has failed you and therefore you had to go to court. It's an indicator of a social breakdown of some sort. So not only are the procedures and what you can expect from enforcement somewhat different, but the cultural attitude in the whole process is completely different.

The Future of Patent Law

I was talking about harmonization a while ago. That's a trend that's going to continue and the reason is because all the big players want it. They want a global playing field where they can get protection across the board and across country boundaries. The large Internet companies will put more pressure on that process, since they are by nature global businesses.

ASPATORE BUSINESS REVIEW
Tear Out This Page and Mail or Fax To:

Aspatore Books, PO Box 883, Bedford, MA 01730
Or Fax To (617) 249-1970

Name:

Email:

Shipping Address:

City: State: Zip:

Billing Address:

City: State: Zip:

Phone:

Lock in at the Current Rates Today-Rates Increase Every Year
Please Check the Desired Length Subscription:

1 Year ($1,090) _____ 2 Years (Save 10%-$1,962) _____
5 Years (Save 20%-$4,360) _____ 10 Years (Save 30%-$7,630) _____
Lifetime Subscription ($24,980) _____

(If mailing in a check you can skip this section but please read fine print below and sign below)
Credit Card Type (Visa & Mastercard & Amex):

Credit Card Number:

Expiration Date:

Signature:

Would you like us to automatically bill your credit card at the end of your subscription so there is no discontinuity in service? (You can still cancel your subscription at any point before the renewal date.) Please circle: Yes No

***(Please note the billing address much match the address on file with your credit card company exactly)**

Terms & Conditions

We shall send a confirmation receipt to your email address. If ordering from Massachusetts, please add 5% sales tax on the order (not including shipping and handling). If ordering from outside of the US, an additional $51.95 per year will be charged for shipping and handling costs. All issues are paperback and will be shipped as soon as they become available. Sorry, no returns or refunds at any point unless automatic billing is selected, at which point you may cancel at any time before your subscription is renewed (no funds shall be returned however for the period currently subscribed to). Issues that are not already published will be shipped upon publication date. Publication dates are subject to delay-please allow 1-2 weeks for delivery of first issue. If a new issue is not coming out for another month, the issue from the previous quarter will be sent for the first issue. For the most up to date information on publication dates and availability please visit www.Aspatore.com.

ORDER THESE OTHER GREAT BOOKS TODAY!

Great for Yourself or Your Entire Team

Visit Your Local Bookseller Today!

Visit www.InsideTheMinds.com For a Complete List of Titles

Bigwig Briefs: The Art of Deal Making (ISBN: 1587621002)
Leading Deal Makers Reveal the Secrets to Negotiating, Leveraging Your Position and Inking Deals - *Bigwig Briefs: The Art of Deal Making* includes knowledge excerpts from some of the biggest name CEOs, Lawyers, VPs of BizDev and Investment Bankers in the world on ways to master the art of deal making. These highly acclaimed deal makers from companies such as Prudential, Credite Suisse First Boston, Barclays, Hogan & Hartson, Proskaur Rose, AT&T and others explain the secrets behind keeping your deal skills sharp, negotiations, working with your team, meetings schedules and environment, deal parameters and other important topics. A must have for every financial professional, lawyer, business development professional, CEO, entrepreneur and individual involved in deal making in any environment and at every level.

Inside the Minds: Leading Marketers (ISBN: 1587620537)
Industry Leaders Share Their Knowledge on the Future of Marketing, Advertising and Building Successful Brands - *Inside the Minds: Leading Marketers* features leading CMOs/EVPs of marketing from General Electric, Federal Express, Coke, Yahoo!, Ford, American Express, Verizon, Major League Baseball and Best Buy. These leading marketers share their knowledge on the future of the marketing industry, the everlasting effects of the Internet and technology, guerrilla marketing, best marketing for the dollars, public relations, advertising, building and sustaining a brand, and other important topics.

Inside the Minds: Chief Technology Officers (ISBN: 1587620081)
Industry Experts Reveal the Secrets to Developing, Implementing, and Capitalizing on the Best Technologies in the World - *Inside the Minds: Chief Technology Officers* features leading technology executives from companies such as Engage, Datek, Symantec, Verisign, Vignette, WebMD, SONICblue, Kana Communications, Flooz.com and The Motley Fool. Their experiences, advice, and research provide an unprecedented look at the various strategies involved with developing, implementing, and capitalizing on the best technologies in the world for companies of every size and in every industry.

Inside the Minds: The Wireless Industry (ISBN: 1587620200)
Industry Leaders Discuss the Future of the Wireless Revolution - *Inside the Minds: The Wireless Industry* features leading CEOs from companies such as AT & T Wireless, Omnisky, Wildblue, AirPrime, Digital Wireless, Aperto Networks, Air2Web, LGC Wireless, Arraycomm, Informio and Extenta. Items discussed include the future of the wireless industry, wireless devices, killer-apps in the wireless industry, the international landscape, government issues and more.

Inside the Minds: Leading Women (ISBN: 1587620197)
What it Takes for Women to Succeed and Have it All in the 21st Century - *Inside the Minds: Leading Women* features CEOs and executives from companies such as Prudential, Women's Financial Network, SiliconSalley.com, Barclays Global Investors, RealEco.com, AgentArts, Kovair, MsMoney.com, LevelEdge and AudioBasket. These

highly acclaimed women explain how to balance personal and professional lives, set goals, network, start a new company, learn the right skills for career advancement and more.

Inside the Minds: Venture Capitalists (ISBN: 1587620014)

Inside the High Stakes and Fast Paced World of Venture Capital - *Inside the Minds: Venture Capitalists* features leading partners from Softbank, ICG, Sequoia Capital, CMGI, New Enterprise Associates, Bertelsmann Ventures, TA Associates, Kestrel Venture Management, Blue Rock Capital, Novak Biddle Venture Partners, Mid-Atlantic Venture Funds, Safeguard Scientific, Divine interVentures, and Boston Capital Ventures. Learn how some of the best minds behind the Internet revolution value companies, assess business models, and identify opportunities in the marketplace.

Inside the Minds: Leading Advertisers (ISBN: 1587620545)

Industry Leaders Share Their Knowledge on the Future of Building Brands Through Advertising – *Inside the Minds: Leading Advertisers* features CEOs/Presidents from agencies such as Young & Rubicam, Leo Burnett, Ogilvy, Saatchi & Saatchi, Interpublic Group, Valassis, Grey Global Group and FCB Worldwide. These leading advertisers share their knowledge on the future of the advertising industry, the everlasting effects of the Internet and technology, client relationships, compensation, building and sustaining brands, and other important topics.

Inside the Minds: Leading Consultants (ISBN: 1587620596)

Industry Leaders Share Their Knowledge on the Future of the Consulting Profession and Industry - *Inside the Minds: Leading Consultants* features leading CEOs/Managing Partners from some of the world's largest consulting companies. These industry leaders share their knowledge on the future of the consulting industry, being an effective team player, the everlasting effects of the Internet and technology, compensation, managing client relationships, motivating others, teamwork, the future of the consulting profession and other important topics.

Inside the Minds: Leading CEOs (ISBN: 1587620553)

Industry Leaders Share Their Knowledge on Management, Motivating Others, and Making a Difference At Any Level Within an Organization - *Inside the Minds: Leading CEOs* features some of the biggest name, proven CEOs in the world. These highly acclaimed CEOs share their knowledge on management, the Internet and technology, client relationships, compensation, motivating others, building and sustaining a profitable business and making a difference at any level within an organization.

Inside the Minds: Internet Marketing (ISBN: 1587620022)

Industry Experts Reveal the Secrets to Marketing, Advertising, and Building a Successful Brand on the Internet - *Inside the Minds: Internet Marketing* features leading marketing VPs from some of the top Internet companies in the world including Buy.com, 24/7 Media, DoubleClick, Guerrilla Marketing, Viant, MicroStrategy, MyPoints.com, WineShopper.com, Advertising.com and eWanted.com. Their experiences, advice, and stories provide an unprecedented look at the various online and offline strategies involved with building a successful brand on the Internet for companies in every industry. Also examined is calculating return on investment, taking an offline brand online, taking an online brand offline, where the future of Internet marketing is heading, and numerous other issues.

Inside the Minds: Internet Bigwigs (ISBN: 1587620103)
Industry Experts Forecast the Future of the Internet Economy (After the Shakedown) - *Inside the Minds: Internet Bigwigs* features a handful of the leading minds of the Internet and technology revolution. These individuals include executives from Excite (Founder), Beenz.com (CEO), Organic (CEO), Agency.com (Founder), Egghead (CEO), Credite Suisse First Boston (Internet Analyst), CIBC (Internet Analyst) and Sandbox.com. Items discussed include killer-apps for the 21st century, the stock market, emerging industries, international opportunities, and a plethora of other issues affecting anyone with a "vested interest" in the Internet and technology revolution.

Bigwig Briefs: Management & Leadership (ISBN: 1587620146)
Industry Experts Reveal the Secrets How to Get There, Stay There, and Empower Others That Work For You
Bigwig Briefs: Management & Leadership includes knowledge excerpts from some of the leading executives in the business world. These highly acclaimed executives explain how to break into higher ranks of management, how to become invaluable to your company, and how to empower your team to perform to their utmost potential.

Bigwig Briefs: The Golden Rules of the Internet Economy (After the Shakedown) (ISBN: 1587620138)
Industry Experts Reveal the Most Important Concepts From the First Phase of the Internet Economy
Bigwig Briefs: The Golden Rules of the Internet Economy includes knowledge excerpts from some of the leading business executives in the Internet and Technology industries. These highly acclaimed executives explain where the future of the Internet economy is heading, mistakes to avoid for companies of all sizes, and the keys to long term success.

Bigwig Briefs: Startups Keys to Success (ISBN: 1587620170)
Industry Experts Reveal the Secrets to Launching a Successful New Venture
Bigwig Briefs: Startups Keys to Success includes knowledge excerpts from some of the leading VCs, CEOs CFOs, CTOs and business executives in every industry. These highly acclaimed executives explain the secrets behind the financial, marketing, business development, legal, and technical aspects of starting a new venture.

Bigwig Briefs: Guerrilla Marketing (ISBN: 1587620677)
The Best of Guerrilla Marketing
Best selling author Jay Levinson shares the now world famous principles behind guerrilla marketing, in the first ever "brief" written on the subject. Items discussed include the Principles Behind Guerrilla Marketing, What Makes a Guerrilla, Attacking the Market, Everyone Is a Marketer, Media Matters, Technology and the Guerrilla Marketer, and Dollars and Sense. A must have for any big time marketing executive, small business owner, entrepreneur, marketer, advertiser, or any one interested in the amazing, proven power of guerrilla marketing.

ASPATORE
BOOKS